Indigenous Women Entrepreneurs in Australia – Shooting for the Stars

This book explores the role of Indigenous identity in entrepreneurial behaviour and success by analysing 14 case studies on Australian Indigenous women entrepreneurs.

The book draws on interviews conducted with successful Indigenous women entrepreneurs who have been operating their businesses across Australia. Each case study is accompanied by relevant literature and industry information to contextualize business challenges and opportunities faced by the individual entrepreneur. The interviews illustrate the intersectional challenge of achieving economic self-determination for Indigenous Women, thereby contributing to a greater understanding of Indigenous entrepreneurship in Australia.

This intersectional study of entrepreneurship will interest students and researchers in the fields of Indigenous studies, entrepreneurship, and anthropology. It will also be a valuable guide for policy makers seeking to promote entrepreneurship amongst Indigenous communities.

Meena Chavan is an Associate Professor of International Business and Entrepreneurship at the Macquarie Business School. She is an economic anthropologist who studies people and business in society to try and understand "what it is to be human in a variety of contexts". She conducts research at the interface of International business & Entrepreneurship. Her research has been published in top-tier ranked journals and books such as Academy of Management Discoveries, Journal of World Business, Journal of International Management, Journal of Business Research, Journal of Small Business Management & Emerald Publications, etc.

Jane Menzies is a supporter of the Indigenous community in Australia. She completed her PhD at Monash University in 2005, on women's participation in international assignments in Multinational Enterprises. Jane is a Senior Lecturer in International Business at the University of Sunshine Coast, and the MBA and Postgraduate Programs coordinator. Her research has been published in top-tier journals such as Journal of Business Research, International Business Review, European Management Journal, Human

Resource Management Review, Management International Review, and others. One of her latest research interests has been on Australian Indigenous Female Entrepreneurship, the subject of this book.

Leanne Holt is a Worimi/Biripi woman from the mid-coast of New South Wales. She is the inaugural Deputy Vice-Chancellor Indigenous at UNSW. Contributing to Indigenous higher education for over 25 years she was previously the inaugural Pro Vice-Chancellor Indigenous Strategy at Macquarie University and prior to this co-director of the Wollotuka Institute at the University of Newcastle. She has a number of publications relating to Indigenous higher education and has been recognised for her leadership, receiving various national and international leadership awards, including being a finalist in the Telstra Women's Business Awards.

Indigenous Women Entrepreneurs in Australia – Shooting for the Stars

Stories of Culture, Resilience and Success

Meena Chavan, Jane Menzies and Leanne Holt

Routledge
Taylor & Francis Group
LONDON AND NEW YORK

First published 2026
by Routledge
4 Park Square, Milton Park, Abingdon, Oxon OX14 4RN

and by Routledge
605 Third Avenue, New York, NY 10158

Routledge is an imprint of the Taylor & Francis Group, an informa business

British Library Cataloguing-in-Publication Data
A catalogue record for this book is available from the British Library

ISBN: 9781032478562 (hbk)
ISBN: 9781032478579 (pbk)
ISBN: 9781003386230 (ebk)

DOI: 10.4324/9781003386230

Typeset in Galliard
by Newgen Publishing UK

Contents

Figures

About the Authors

Associate Professor Meena Chavan

Meena Chavan is an Associate Professor of International Business and Entrepreneurship at the Macquarie Business School. As an Economic Anthropologist, she studies how human societies sustain themselves through production, distribution, exchange, and consumption within specific societal contexts, comparing these practices across different times and places, and analysing historical patterns of economic organization.

She conducts research to study Entrepreneurship amongst people from diverse communities and life spaces like immigrant ethnic, refugees and the Indigenous community internationally that lead to the creation of successful enterprises that contribute to the betterment of society.

She has published in top-tier journals like Academy of Management, Journal of World Business, Small Business Journal, and Journal of International Management.

Her 2021 book *Intercultural management in practice—Learning to lead diverse global organisations,* Emerald Publications, Australia, helps modern-day business leaders to manage diverse global organisations and teams that work in international contexts. This book assists organisations of all types to manage diversity and promote inclusion in their national and international operations and markets.

Her 2022 book, *Exploring the Economic Opportunities and Impacts of Migrant Entrepreneurship: Success Stories and Case Studies*, acquaints the reader with high-performing successful international entrepreneurs in Australia.

Dr Jane Menzies

Jane Menzies is a female academic and supporter of the Indigenous community in Australia. She is positive about the strong contribution that Indigenous businesses can make to the Australian economy. She completed her PhD at Monash University in 2005, on women's participation in international assignments in Multinational Enterprises. Her research interests are in internationalisation of firms, women's entrepreneurship, and gender issues in organisations. One of her latest research interests has been on Australian

Indigenous Female Entrepreneurship, the subject of this book. Jane has published in *Critical Perspectives on International Business, Journal of Business Research, International Business Review, European Management Journal, Thunderbird International Business Review, Academy of International Business Insights, International Journal of Consumer Studies, International Journal of Conflict Management, Management International Review, Human Resource Management Review, International Trade Journal, European Business Review, Australian Journal of Career Development*, and a range of education journals. Jane published a book with Routledge in 2018 on 'Innovation and Internationalisation: Australian SMEs in China.' Jane has over the years been awarded grants at the Australia China Council (2013) and more recently at the Council for Australia Latin America Relations (2022), both at the Department of Foreign Affairs and Trade.

Professor Leanne Holt

Leanne Holt is a Worimi/Biripi woman from the mid-coast of New South Wales. She is the inaugural Deputy Vice-Chancellor Indigenous at UNSW. Contributing to Indigenous higher education for over 25 years, she was previously the inaugural Pro Vice-Chancellor Indigenous Strategy at Macquarie University and prior to this co-Director of the Wollotuka Institute at the University of Newcastle.

Professor Holt's qualifications began in human resources going on to complete postgraduate programs in Business and Management. In 2016, she was awarded a PhD (Education) from the University of Newcastle, for her thesis titled Development of Aboriginal Education Policy in Australia: Voices of the National Aboriginal Education Committee.

Professor Holt has chaired and been a member of a number of national and international Indigenous education committees. She is currently Chairperson of Yadhu Maru and Universities Australia DVC Indigenous Committee, as well as Board member of Barabarang Aboriginal Corporation and Barang Alliance. Professor Holt is additionally a member of expert panels including the Department of Education Equity in Higher Education Panel and the Australian Centre for Access and Success Advisory Board. She is an expert panel member for the Tertiary Education and Quality Standards Authority (TEQSA) and has chaired a number of panels reviewing Indigenous programs and services at universities nationally and internationally.

Professor Holt is the author of the book 'Talking Strong' and is Chief Investigator on Australian Research Council, Medical Research Future Fund, Ministry of Health and other Indigenous education and health related research projects. She has a number of publications relating to Indigenous higher education and has been recognised for her leadership receiving various national and international leadership awards, including being a finalist in the Telstra Women's Business Awards.

Foreword – Celebrating Resilience, Innovation, and Entrepreneurship

Professor Leanne Holt

It is with immense pride that I introduce this inspiring work—an homage to the entrepreneurial spirit of Australian Indigenous women. This book highlights the stories of strength, determination, and unwavering resilience that have defined these women's journeys.

Indigenous women have long been the foundation of their communities—mothers, sisters, aunties, and grandmothers who shape and preserve the cultural fabric of Australia. Yet, their entrepreneurial endeavours have often remained overlooked, overshadowed by systemic challenges, historical injustices, and the lasting effects of colonization, displacement, and dispossession.

This book seeks to change that narrative. It brings forward the voices of trailblazing Indigenous women—visionaries who have defied the odds, shattered glass ceilings, and forged their own paths. Their businesses span various fields—fashion, culture, food, music, film, consulting, health, and more—but all are united by a common thread: resilience.

As you read their stories of triumph and perseverance, remember that each one carries a lesson. These women have faced adversity, overcome obstacles, and transformed challenges into opportunities. Their courage inspires us all to dream bigger, work harder, and drive change.

To the aspiring entrepreneurs reading this: you too can make a difference. Whether you are launching a small venture or dreaming of global impact, know that while the path may be difficult, it is worth every step. Seek mentors, build networks, and embrace your unique perspective.

May these stories ignite your entrepreneurial spirit and remind you that innovation and entrepreneurship are boundless, transcending race and gender. However, we must also create structures at societal, governmental, community, interpersonal, and individual levels that support Australian Indigenous women in their entrepreneurial pursuits. Let these stories empower you to take that first bold step toward building your own legacy.

Acknowledgements

We would like to sincerely thank our respondents who have provided us with their valuable time and given us interesting and valuable insights into the fascinating world of Indigenous Women Entrepreneurship.

We would also like to thank Dr Rob Jack of Macquarie Business School and Dr Simona Scarparo of Deakin University who were instrumental in interviewing some candidates.

Our thanks also go to the research assistants:
Angela Dela Cruz, Research intern, Macquarie University
Bailey Deng, Research intern, Macquarie University
Georgette Borel, Research intern, Macquarie University

1 Australian Indigenous Women Entrepreneurs: Shooting for the Stars

First Nations Female Entrepreneurs in Australia: Stories of Culture, Resilience and Success

Meena Chavan, Jane Menzies, and Leanne Holt

Introduction, Theoretical frameworks and setting the scene

Research on Australian Indigenous Female Entrepreneurs (AIFE) is limited, with only a handful of studies conducted over the past three decades. However, with the strengthening of Indigenous rights in Australia and the advocacy for "A Voice to Parliament" in 2023 (Reconciliation Australia, 2023), it is now timely and critical to explore the experiences of Indigenous women who are establishing and running entrepreneurial businesses. Moreover, much of the existing literature is dated, raising questions about its relevance in today's increasingly digital business landscape.

This book addresses these concerns by focusing on Australian Indigenous Female Entrepreneurs (AIFEs). It shares the stories of 14 Indigenous women who have successfully established businesses across Australia. Throughout history, women have held vital roles within Aboriginal and Torres Strait Islander communities, serving as mothers, sisters, aunties, and grandmothers, deeply respected for their contributions to the social, cultural, environmental, and economic fabric of Australia. Despite their vast strengths, skills, and knowledge, Aboriginal women continue to face systemic exclusion, positioning them as one of the most marginalized groups in Australia. The stories in this book shed light on the challenges and opportunities faced by Australian Indigenous Female Entrepreneurs, celebrating their resilience and achievements against adversity.

It is crucial to recognize, support, and empower these women, enabling them to control their own economic development—an essential component of self-determination (Murphy, 2014). By sharing their stories, we offer insights for other Aboriginal women to follow in their footsteps and develop successful entrepreneurial ventures. This book offers a unique opportunity to learn about Indigenous entrepreneurship from an Australian perspective through real-life case studies of successful Indigenous women in various fields.

DOI: 10.4324/9781003386230-1

The book serves as an invaluable resource for students of entrepreneurship and Indigenous studies, while also offering policymakers important insights on how to promote entrepreneurship within Indigenous communities. Additionally, it is an inspiring guide for other women considering entrepreneurship. A book focused on Australian Indigenous women entrepreneurs is significant for several reasons: it amplifies their voices and experiences, provides educational resources for future generations, and contributes to a more inclusive and equitable society where diverse perspectives are celebrated.

Background of Australian Indigenous Peoples

In 2021, the Australian Bureau of Statistics reported an Indigenous population of approximately 881,600 people (AIHW, 2022). Aboriginal and Torres Strait Islander peoples are the Indigenous people of Australia, representing hundreds of distinct cultural groups across the country. As the AIHW (2022) highlights, these groups possess their own languages, traditions, and cultural practices. Projections suggest the Indigenous population in Australia will reach 1.1 million by 2031 (Australian Bureau of Statistics, 2019), indicating that more Indigenous people will be seeking employment opportunities and establishing entrepreneurial ventures. This book is both timely and informative for those seeking to engage in self-determination and economic prosperity.

The Indigenous population is geographically spread across Australia: 38% live in capital cities, 44% in inner and outer regional areas, and 17% in remote or very remote communities (Australian Bureau of Statistics, 2019). Additionally, the Indigenous population is notably young, with an average age of 23, suggesting that many will soon be seeking employment or business opportunities (Australian Bureau of Statistics, 2019). With this in mind, frameworks and strategies to support Indigenous women in establishing and running successful businesses are imperative

Background of Indigenous Entrepreneurship

Indigenous entrepreneurship in Australia has a rich and ancient history, stretching back over 50,000 years. During this period, Indigenous communities engaged in trade, labor, and cultural exchange. Indigenous clans enhanced their traditional practices with activities such as hunting, fishing, horticulture, and gathering, which were essential for survival (Pearson & Daff, 2014). Written records reveal that Indigenous people from Arnhem Land, Northern Territory, participated in trade with seafarers as early as the 17th century. Notably, the Yolngu people of North Arnhem Land traded pearls, turtle shells, fish, and trepang (sea cucumber) with the Macassans from present-day Indonesia, exchanging these goods for steel, axes, cloth, tobacco, and alcohol (Macknight, 1986; Trudgen, 2000; Worsley, 1955). These trade relationships fostered not only the exchange of goods but also cultural understanding. Indigenous entrepreneurs demonstrated adaptability, resilience, and resource management skills, overcoming various challenges, including colonization and dispossession.

Today, Indigenous entrepreneurs continue to build upon this legacy, navigating the complexities of modern business landscapes. Research shows that many Indigenous women entrepreneurs hold formal qualifications, are proficient in business regulations, and maintain their own websites. They often speak multiple languages, further enriching their entrepreneurial capacity (Pearson & Daff, 2014).

Motivations for this Book and Study

Associate Professor Meena Chavan's motivation to write this book, *Indigenous Women Entrepreneurs: Shooting for the Stars*, stems from her research on diverse entrepreneurs in Australia and her close work with the Walanga Muru, Indigenous unit at Macquarie University. Macquarie University acknowledges and respects the vital contributions of Aboriginal and Torres Strait Islander peoples, aligning with their Indigenous research plan, which promotes research that highlights Indigenous knowledge and perspectives. Meena has long been connected with the Indigenous community and has been inspired by the stories and lives of Indigenous women in Australia, guiding her research in Indigenous culture and entrepreneurship.

Dr. Jane Menzies' interest in Indigenous entrepreneurship grew through her academic involvement and the ongoing push within Australian universities to promote Indigenous strategies. The global social movements, such as Black Lives Matter, along with her research on women's entrepreneurship, led to a collaboration with Dr. Chavan to explore the experiences of First Nations women entrepreneurs.

Professor Leanne Holt, Deputy Vice-Chancellor Indigenous, has dedicated her career to advancing Indigenous education and empowerment. As a Worimi/Biripi woman, her commitment to amplifying the voices of Indigenous women stems from honoring the legacy of her ancestors—women who were leaders, carers, educators, and entrepreneurs. She views this book as an opportunity to celebrate their enduring legacy and inspire future generations of Indigenous women to pursue their entrepreneurial aspirations, knowing they stand on the shoulders of trailblazers who have overcome great adversity.

Previous Literature on Australian Indigenous Female Entrepreneurs

Indigenous female entrepreneurship in Australia is often defined as "Indigenous women starting, managing, and growing their own businesses" (Menzies et al., 2024; Menzies, 2020). However, as noted by Wood and Davidson (2011), there is a notable lack of comprehensive literature on Australian Indigenous female entrepreneurs (AIFEs), and this gap remains evident in the literature through to 2024. Their research highlighted the distinctive barriers faced by AIFEs that are not experienced by their non-Indigenous counterparts, including racial discrimination, prejudice, alienation from their own Indigenous communities, limited formal education, and a clash of cultural values. Other identified obstacles include the absence of role models, language barriers, and limited access to finance and networks (Wood & Davidson, 2011). The study also highlighted that AIFEs are often motivated to start businesses as a means to escape poverty, improve their quality of life, elevate their social status, and promote self-determination and economic empowerment (Wood & Davidson, 2011).

In addition to these barriers, Davis (1992) emphasized that Indigenous women frequently take leadership roles in decision-making within their communities. While Australian Indigenous women have historically been underrepresented in entrepreneurship, it is crucial to recognize the potential impact of their businesses on economic growth, self-determination, and development within their communities. AIFEs are creating and managing enterprises in diverse industries, contributing to the Australian economy and society with innovative products, services, and ideas. Prominent examples of AIFEs include businesses in sectors like Indigenous modeling agencies, jewellery, food products, and more (Foley, 2020; Pascoe & Taylor, 2020; Tu, 2020). A study by Dana (1995) found that many AIFE-led businesses are in retail clothing, arts and crafts, childcare, beauty salons, and professional services, with many of these women being single mothers (Dana, 1995). These AIFEs are making significant contributions to their communities and serve as role models for the next generation of Indigenous women leaders and entrepreneurs.

The literature further indicates that AIFEs face unique challenges, including difficulties accessing capital, overcoming cultural and gender-based biases, and navigating complex regulatory frameworks (Pearson & Daff, 2014). Despite these challenges, they bring distinctive strengths to entrepreneurship, such as a deep understanding of their culture, environment, and communities. Indigenous entrepreneurs are recognized as critical agents of change, advancing not only economic growth but also social and environmental sustainability. Many of their businesses prioritize social or environmental goals alongside profit generation. AIFEs are represented across various industries, including recruitment, fashion, food, tourism, consulting, cultural training, and the arts (Pearce, 2015).

The literature acknowledges that Indigenous women face historical and gendered discrimination, making their entrepreneurial journey more challenging (Allui & Park, 2024; Wood & Davidson, 2011). Factors such as limited access to resources, education, and training contribute to these challenges. One potential solution to address these barriers is to support the economic development, financial literacy, and entrepreneurial skills of Indigenous women. While the body of literature examining Indigenous female entrepreneurship in Australia has expanded, there remains a significant gap in research. Key studies, such as those by Pearson and Daff (2014), have explored Indigenous women entrepreneurs in remote locations. They found that Indigenous cultures remain patriarchal, and female entrepreneurs often adapt their businesses to comply with Australian regulations while maintaining cultural sensitivity to traditional norms (Pearson & Daff, 2014). However, there is still limited research on this topic, despite the fact that the Indigenous business sector contributes significantly to the Australian economy, generating $16 billion in 2024 and employing over 116,000 people (Prestipino, 2024).

AIFEs are often based in urban areas but continue to face challenges related to socio-economic disadvantage, particularly in remote regions. As Pearson and Daff (2014) noted, many AIFEs aim to create businesses that reflect their cultural values while adhering to government regulations. Some of these businesses involve practices such as wildlife harvesting and organizing cultural or religious events.

Pearson and Daff (2014) also found that many AIFEs started their businesses out of necessity, as they faced financial hardship and relied on welfare. These women often used art or other cultural practices to generate supplementary income. For many, their entrepreneurial ventures were not about building wealth but about gaining financial independence and reducing reliance on government support. Cultural and social motivators, such as maintaining kinship obligations, preserving cultural heritage, and contributing to their community, were also significant drivers for these entrepreneurs (Pearson & Daff, 2014). For example, artist-entrepreneurs often sought to share their culture, tell their stories, and preserve their traditions through their work.

Despite these cultural motivators, AIFEs face resource barriers such as limited access to capital, transportation issues, and challenges in market access (Pearson & Daff, 2014). In some cases, cultural barriers such as hierarchical kinship structures, gender-based expectations, and family obligations also impact their ability to run businesses. Additionally, the prevalence of male violence in some communities can hinder women's entrepreneurial efforts. McDonnell (1999) found that many Indigenous women lack access to traditional forms of credit, limiting their ability to expand their businesses. Consequently, there is a strong demand for culturally appropriate financial services to support Indigenous entrepreneurs.

Pearson and Daff (2014) describe the need for AIFEs to navigate a unique set of challenges, referred to as "cross-vergence." They must reconcile traditional cultural values and norms with the pressures to conform to modern business regulations, such as taxation and compliance. These women are often embedded in patriarchal clan structures, but some Indigenous cultures are matriarchal, offering a different experience for women in those communities. The relationship between Indigenous culture and entrepreneurship is complex and sometimes contradictory. Factors such as racial discrimination, socio-economic disadvantage, and the blending of Indigenous and non-Indigenous cultural practices further complicate their entrepreneurial journeys.

Collins et al. (2017) explored the experiences of 16 female Indigenous entrepreneurs compared with 22 male counterparts and found that male entrepreneurs were more likely to have non-Indigenous partners. For some women, having a non-Indigenous partner provided access to valuable resources such as human, social, and economic capital. These women often experienced less gender discrimination than those with Indigenous partners. However, AIFEs often approach their businesses with a strong cultural foundation, guided by values such as kinship, respect for Elders, and cultural integrity. Their businesses are shaped by their cultural heritage and serve to promote cultural awareness, maintain family relationships, and strengthen their communities.

The Impact of Indigenous Culture on AIFE Ventures

Cultural factors play a significant role in the establishment and growth of Indigenous businesses. Key cultural elements include:

- Connection to country
- Caring for country
- Self-determination
- Family and kinship
- Cultural expression (AIHW, 2022; Bourke et al., 2018)

Indigenous culture emphasizes the transmission of knowledge, traditions, ceremonies, and stories across generations, often through language, art, and the guidance of Elders (Bourke et al., 2018). Collins et al. (2017) found that culture can either enable or constrain business ventures. For example, businesses rooted in Indigenous culture, such as those in tourism or the arts, benefit from cultural knowledge and traditions. However, cultural constraints may arise if Indigenous workers are not available, or if mainstream businesses refuse to engage with AIFEs. Collins et al. (2017) identified four key themes related to culture in Indigenous entrepreneurship:

1. **Family and Kinship Priorities**: A strong sense of responsibility toward family and community.
2. **Egalitarianism**: A commitment to fairness and equity.
3. **Survivor Mentality**: A collective strength and resilience developed through the history of colonization.
4. **Cultural Knowledge Products and Services**: The promotion of Indigenous culture through art, food, and storytelling.

These themes reflect the values that shape AIFEs and underscore their role in both economic and cultural preservation.

Given the insights from prior research, it is clear that while Indigenous female entrepreneurship has received growing attention, there is still a significant need for further exploration. This includes both updating existing literature with more recent accounts of AIFEs and examining their entrepreneurial journeys in the face of ongoing adversity. The following section details the methods used in this study to further our understanding of AIFEs and their contributions to the Australian economy and society.

Study Overview and Methodology

This research employed a qualitative approach, consisting of interviews with 18 Indigenous Female Entrepreneurs (AIFEs). However, only 15 of these participants consented to include their stories in this publication. Qualitative research is centered on the systematic collection and analysis of a range of empirical materials that capture everyday experiences, challenges, and the meanings individuals attach to them. This type of research explores phenomena within their natural context, seeking to interpret and understand the meanings people assign to them (Denzin & Lincoln, 2018). To present our findings, we utilized case studies to offer in-depth insights into the participants' experiences.

Qualitative research is particularly effective for examining novel, underexplored, or hard-to-quantify entrepreneurial phenomena (Van Burg et al., 2022). A critical aspect of this research was the "connection" between the researcher and the entrepreneur. When an organization reflects the values and vision of its founder, establishing a meaningful rapport with the founder is essential for uncovering insights and understanding their true experiences. This connection allows researchers to explore deeper insights, identify hidden aspects of the entrepreneurial journey, and ask difficult yet necessary questions (Baker, Powell & Flutz, 2017).

Grounded theory, the predominant method for theory development in entrepreneurship research, served as the backbone of our study (Glaser & Strauss, 1967). It is often regarded as the quintessential approach for qualitative research in entrepreneurship (Suddaby et al., 2015; Van Burg et al., 2022). Our data, derived from the stories of Indigenous female entrepreneurs, sheds light on their motivations, challenges, and successes in navigating their entrepreneurial journeys. Grounded theory was chosen because it promotes reflexivity and allows for a deep understanding of participants' lived experiences, especially in unfamiliar or underexplored contexts (Leedy et al., 2014). This methodology also enables researchers to identify the themes and connections participants attribute to their entrepreneurial experiences.

Given the interpretive nature of this research, we employed an approach that prioritizes the perspectives and lived realities of the participants (Dacin et al., 2010). In addressing interpretive challenges, many researchers rely on structured templates, such as Gioia's methodology, which is widely accepted for conducting interpretive qualitative research (Gioia et al., 2022). This approach views interviewees as knowledgeable agents, capable of articulating their thoughts and actions (Gioia et al., 2013). It advocates an inductive approach, where researchers prioritize the data and the participants' language before drawing any theoretical conclusions (Van Burg et al., 2022).

Following the guidelines of Glaser & Strauss (1967), we initially set aside existing literature to allow a model to emerge directly from the data. This process allowed us to generate theories grounded in the participants' narratives, rather than imposing pre-existing theoretical frameworks. Existing theoretical knowledge was, however, used to inform initial questions during early interviews and observations (Strauss & Corbin, 1998). We employed a constant comparison method for data collection, coding, and analysis, continuing this process until we reached data saturation—when no new insights were emerging (Strauss & Corbin, 1998).

Research Context and Sample

We utilized purposive sampling to select participants (Gartner & Birley, 2002; Pratt, 2009). Indigenous women entrepreneurs were identified through LinkedIn and 'Supply Nation,' a database of Indigenous businesses. After securing contact details, we sent email invitations outlining the research aims and inviting participation in semi-structured interviews. Out of the 30 individuals approached, 24 agreed to participate. Ultimately, 14 participants were selected based on the suitability of their business experiences, particularly those who had been operating for a minimum of five years. These participants represented a diverse range of industries.

Interviews and Archival Data

Semi-structured face-to-face interviews were conducted, each lasting between 45 to 60 minutes. All interviews were audio-recorded and transcribed verbatim. The first round of interviews continued until data saturation was achieved, marked by a repetition of responses (Boddy, 2016; Creswell & Creswell, 2017). Follow-up interviews, lasting 15 to 20 minutes, were conducted via telephone. During these follow-up interviews, participants were informed that their transcribed interviews would be sent to them for review and approval (Bell et al., 2018). Additionally, informal discussions were held to clarify any remaining questions.

Supplementary data were gathered from secondary sources such as internal documents, company websites, and archival materials. Researchers also attended informal meetings, social interactions, and workshops facilitated by the participants. These observations contributed to a deeper understanding of the entrepreneurial contexts. The research team regularly discussed the data, refining our interviewing techniques and enhancing the overall analysis. We also analyzed governmental reports, media articles, and newsletters from Indigenous entrepreneurship incubators.

Analytical Approach

We applied inductive analysis to the qualitative data, adhering to the constant comparison technique for grounded theory (Glaser & Strauss, 1967; Strauss & Corbin, 1990). Our analysis consisted of four stages. The first stage involved open coding of the initial 18 interviews, which were analyzed in detail using a line-by-line coding approach (Strauss & Corbin, 1990). These initial codes formed the first-order codes, which were then used to analyze subsequent interview transcripts. New codes were introduced as necessary. Next, we grouped these first-order codes into broader second-order themes, which were then linked to theoretical concepts within the field. The results of this analysis are presented in the following chapters, where we explore the entrepreneurial journeys of the AIFEs.

Structure of the Book

Foreword
Chapter 1: Introduction, theoretical frameworks and setting the scene
Chapter 2: Mundanara Bayles
Chapter 3: Jennifer Daar
Chapter 4: Nicole Monks
Chapter 5: Nicole Brown
Chapter 6: Kaylene Langford
Chapter 7: Rebecca Wessels
Chapter 8: Carol Vale
Chapter 9: Rachelle Towart
Chapter 10: Amanda Healy
Chapter 11: Fran Dobbie
Chapter 12- Denni Francisco
Chapter 13: Judith McDonald
Chapter 14: Vattessa Colbung
Chapter 15: Janine McDonald
Chapter 16: Lessons Learned, Policy Implications and Conclusions

References

AIHW. (2022). *Profile of Indigenous Australians.* Retrieved 05/05/22 from www.aihw.gov.au/reports/australias-welfare/profile-of-indigenous-australians

Australian Bureau of Statistics. (2019). *Estimates and Projections, Aboriginal and Torres Strait Islander Australians.* Australian Government. Retrieved 19/04/2023 from www.abs.gov.au/statistics/people/aboriginal-and-torres-strait-islander-peoples/estimates-and-projections-aboriginal-and-torres-strait-islander-australians/latest-release

Baker, Ted & Welter, Friederike. (2018). Contextual Entrepreneurship: An Interdisciplinary Perspective. Foundations and Trends® in Entrepreneurship. 14. 357-426. 10.1561/0300000078.
Bell, E., Bryman, A., & Harley, B. (2018). *Business Research Methods*. Oxford University Press.
Boddy, C. R. (2016). Sample size for qualitative research. *Qualitative Market Research: An International Journal*, *19*(4), 426–432. https://doi.org/10.1108/QMR-06-2016-0053
Bourke, S., Wright, A., Guthrie, J., Russell, L., Dunbar, T., & Lovett, R. (2018). Evidence review of indigenous culture for health and wellbeing. *The International Journal of Health, Wellness, and Society*, *8*(4), 11–27. doi:10.18848/2156-8960/CGP/v08i04/11-27
Collins, J., Morrison, M., Basu, P. K., & Krivokapic-Skoko, B. (2017). Indigenous culture and entrepreneurship in small businesses in Australia. *Small Enterprise Research*, *24*(1), 36–48. https://doi.org/10.1080/13215906.2017.1289855
Creswell, J. W., & Creswell, J. D. (2017). *Research Design: Qualitative, Quantitative, and Mixed Methods Approaches* (4th ed.). Sage Publications.
Dacin, Tina & Dacin, Peter & Tracey, Paul. (2011). Social Entrepreneurship: *A Critique and Future Directions*. Organization Science. 22. 1203–1213. 10.2307/41303113.
Dana, L.-P. (1995). Entrepreneurship in a remote Sub-Arctic community. *Entrepreneurship Theory and Practice*, *20*(1), 57–72. https://doi.org/10.1177/104225879502000104
Davis, M. (2012). Aboriginal women: The right to self-determination. *Australian Indigenous Law Review*, *16*(1), 78–88. https://search.informit.org/doi/10.3316/ielapa.300012026243154.
Denzin, N. K., & Lincoln, Y. S. (Eds.). (2018). *The SAGE Handbook of Qualitative Research* (5th ed.). Los Angeles, CA: Sage.
Foley, D. (2020). *9 Indigenous startup founders changing Australian entrepreneurship*. www.startupdaily.net/topic/people/9-indigenous-startup-founders-changing-australian-entrepreneurship/
Gale, T. (2024). *An examination of the lived experiences of Indigenous women in elite and sub-elite Australian rules football and rugby league*. [Doctoral Thesis, Charles Sturt University]. Charles Sturt University
Gartner, W. B., & Birley, S. (2002). *Introduction to the Special Issue on Qualitative Methods in Entrepreneurship Research*. Elsevier.
Gioia, D.A., Corley, K.G. and Hamilton, A.L. (2013) *Seeking Qualitative Rigor in Inductive Research: Notes on the Gioia Methodology*. Organizational Research Methods, 16, 15–31. https://doi.org/10.1177/1094428112452151.
Gioia, D., Corley, K., Eisenhardt, K., Feldman, M., Langley, A., Lê, J., Golden-Biddle, K., Locke, K., Mees-Buss, J., Piekkari, R., Ravasi, D., Rerup, C., Schmid, T., Silverman, D., & Welch, C. (2022). A Curated Debate: On Using "Templates" in Qualitative Research. *Journal of Management Inquiry*, *31*(3), 231–252. https://doi.org/10.1177/10564926221098955 (Original work published 2022
Glaser, B., & Strauss, A. (1967). The Discovery of Grounded Theory: *Strategies for Qualitative Research*. Mill Valley, CA: Sociology Press.
Leedy, P. D., Ormrod, J. E., & Johnson, L. R. (2014). *Practical Research: Planning and Design*. Pearson Education.

Macknight, C. C. (1986). Macassans and the Aboriginal Past. *Archaeology in Oceania, 21*(1), 69–75. www.jstor.org/stable/40386713

McDonnell, Siobhan --- "Giving Credit Where It's Due: The Operation of Micro - Credit Models in an Indigenous Australian Context" [2001] IndigLawB 69; (2001) 5(12) Indigenous Law Bulletin 6.

Menzies, J. (2020). *Promoting Indigenous Affairs within Organisations.* Deakin University. Retrieved 19/02/2023 from https://businessnewsroom.deakin.edu.au/articles/promoting-indigenous-affairs-within-organisations-ngata

Menzies, J., Chavan, M., Jack, R., Scarparo, S., & Chirico, F. (2024). Australian indigenous female entrepreneurs: The role of adversity quotient. *Journal of Business Research, 175*, 114558. https://doi.org/https://doi.org/10.1016/j.jbusres.2024.114558

Murphy, M. (2014). Self-determination as a collective capability: The case of indigenous peoples. *Journal of Human Development and Capabilities, 15*(4), 320–334. https://doi.org/10.1080/19452829.2013.878320

Pascoe, A., & Taylor, L. (2020). *6 Indigenous-Owned Businesses To Get Behind Immediately.* www.marieclaire.com.au/indigenous-businesses-australia

Pearce, Philip L. (2015) *Understanding and fostering intelligent tourist behaviour.* Tourism Tribune, 30 (11). pp. 5–9.

Pearson, C. A. L., & Daff, S. (2014). Female Indigenous entrepreneurship in remote communities in northern Australia. *Information Management and Business Review, 6*(6), 329–344.

Pratt, A. C. (2009). Urban regeneration: From the artsfeel good'factor to the cultural economy: A case study of Hoxton, London. *Urban Studies, 46*(5–6), 1041–1061.

Prestipino, D. (2024). *Indigenous businesses hit $10b milestone with spending tipped to skyrocket.* Retrieved 23/01/2025 from https://nit.com.au/01-10-2024/13997/indigenous-businesses-hit-10b-milestone-with-spending-tipped-to-skyrocket#:~:text=The%20First%20Nations%20business%20sector,them%20upwards%20of%20%244b.

Reconciliation Australia. (2023). *Large, diverse support for the Voice to Parliament.* Retrieved 10 June 2024 from www.reconciliation.org.au/large-diverse-support-for-the-voice-to-parliament/

Strauss, A., & Corbin, J. (1998). *Basics of qualitative research: Techniques and procedures for developing grounded theory* (2nd ed.). Sage Publications, Inc.

Strauss, A., & Corbin, J. M. (1990). *Basics of qualitative research: Grounded theory procedures and techniques.* Sage Publications, Inc.

Suddaby, Roy & Bruton, Garry D. & Si, Steven X., 2015. "Entrepreneurship through a qualitative lens: Insights on the construction and/or discovery of entrepreneurial opportunity," *Journal of Business Venturing*, Elsevier, 30(1), 1–10.

Trudgen, R. (2000). *Why Warriors lie down & die: Towards an Understanding of why the Aboriginal People of Arnhem Land face the Greatest Crisis in Health and Education since European Contact: Djambatj Mala.* Aboriginal Resource & Development Services Inc.

Tu, J. (2020). *10 Indigenous women blazing a trail in Australia today.* https://womensagenda.com.au/latest/10-indigenous-women-blazing-a-trail-in-australia-today/

Van Burg, E., Cornelissen, J., Stam, W., & Jack, S. (2020). Advancing Qualitative Entrepreneurship Research: Leveraging Methodological Plurality for Achieving Scholarly Impact. *Entrepreneurship Theory and Practice, 46*(1), 3–20. https://doi.org/10.1177/1042258720943051.

Wood, G.J. and Davidson, M.J. (2011), "A review of male and female Australian indigenous entrepreneurs: Disadvantaged past – promising future?", *Gender in Management*, 26 (4), pp. 311–326. https://doi.org/10.1108/17542411111144319

Worsley, P. (1955). 63. The Totemic System of the WaniNdijaugwa. *Man*, 55, 57. https://doi.org/10.2307/2795208

2 Mundanara Bayles

https://theblackcard.com.au/mundanarabayles

Meena Chavan, Jane Menzies, and Leanne Holt

Mundanara Bayles is the Co-founder and Managing Director of BlackCard Pty. Ltd. (www.theblackcard.com.au/), a 100% Aboriginal-owned business she established alongside her great aunt, Dr. Lilla Watson. BlackCard specializes in building cultural capability training and consultancy, empowering individuals and organizations to work more effectively with Aboriginal and Torres Strait Islander peoples. The business is certified with Supply Nation, an Australian government initiative that champions Indigenous enterprises. With over two decades of experience across the community, not-for-profit (NFP), and government sectors in New South Wales and Queensland, Mundanara has built a strong foundation for advocating for Aboriginal and Torres Strait Islander rights and creating positive change.

Early and Personal Life

Mundanara Bayles is a proud Koori woman, a mother of five, and married to a Fijian Kiwi. She resides on Kabi Kabi Country, also known as the Sunshine Coast. Mundanara's heritage spans the Birri-Gubba (North Queensland) and Gungalu people of the Dawson River (Central Queensland) through her father, and the Wonnarua people of the Hunter Valley, Bunjalung, and Gweagal peoples through her mother.

Raised in Redfern, Sydney, alongside her eight sisters in a politically active family, Mundanara's childhood was immersed in the fight for Aboriginal rights and equality. Her father, Tiga Bayles, an Aboriginal activist, was deeply involved in the protest movements of the 1970s. In 1990, the family relocated to Brisbane after Tiga received an opportunity to work at Triple A Murri Country, an Aboriginal community radio station founded by her great-uncle, Ross Watson. This relocation brought her to the Murri School, Brisbane's only Aboriginal community school, founded by her late uncle. Mundanara graduated from the Murri School and went on to serve for over ten years as a director on the Murri School Board.

Mundanara's family legacy extends beyond education; they also helped establish healthcare services, legal aid, and community connections such as

DOI: 10.4324/9781003386230-2

Link-Up, which helps reunite the Stolen Generations with their families. Her great aunt, Lilla Watson, was a key figure in the early years of the Aboriginal Child Care Agency, which garnered respect within the local Aboriginal community. Tiga Bayles also founded Radio Redfern, now known as Koori Radio, which continues to operate today.

Growing up, Mundanara felt the weight of her family's history and the expectations that came with it. "It comes with a lot of responsibility, and there's a lot of pressure. As a young person, I always felt it was unfair that I couldn't just go into a nightclub and have a good time because people were watching me," she recalls. Despite this, Mundanara embraces the responsibility that comes with her family name. "I want my children to be able to walk into communities right across this country and be able to tell mob who they are, who their grandfather was, and be welcomed with open arms."

Her personal life is enriched by her husband and their five children. Living in Mount Coolum, Gubbi Gubbi Country, they enjoy a peaceful home surrounded by the second-largest rock formation in Australia, which Mundanara describes as a magical place. However, Redfern remains her true home. "I love where we live, but Redfern will always be my home," she says.

Mundanara has continued her father's legacy, particularly in advocating for Aboriginal rights. Her father became the inaugural Chairperson of the New South Wales State Aboriginal Land Council at just 29. His dedication to building community relationships, despite the lack of financial compensation, is a source of inspiration for her. "Dad knew everyone. Word traveled quickly in the Aboriginal community. He had eyes everywhere," she reflects.

Her mother's side of the family experienced deep intergenerational trauma, exacerbated by the Stolen Generations and systemic injustice. Her mother passed away at just 45 years old, a victim of the compounded effects of this trauma. Mundanara emphasizes the importance of educating Australians about the true history of the country. "We need to shake up especially white Australians. We need them to learn the history of this country—it's not Aboriginal history, it's Australian history, our shared history," she urges. Mundanara uses her personal experiences to inform her work, often sharing her story to underscore the statistics she presents in her cultural competence training.

Professional Life and Career

By the age of 18, Mundanara had already faced significant challenges, including the sudden passing of her mother and the responsibility of caring for her sister's four children while her sister served time in prison. This experience was not unique in her family, as several of her sisters faced incarceration and teenage motherhood. Despite these personal challenges, Mundanara worked at a youth detention center in Brisbane, where she supported young people, many of whom she had attended school with at the Murri School.

At 19, she began working with a group training organization in South Brisbane, helping Aboriginal and Torres Strait Islander students secure apprenticeships and traineeships. Despite being the only Aboriginal employee, Mundanara persevered in her work, even as she navigated cultural isolation and discrimination. "I was constantly being asked to justify my Aboriginality," she recalls, often facing racial remarks and microaggressions. This experience, unfortunately, is one shared by many Aboriginal people in the workforce.

Her persistence in the face of adversity led her to entrepreneurship, a path she initially resisted but was ultimately forced into for survival. The frequent racism and lack of cultural understanding in her workplaces became untenable, and she recognized the need to build something of her own. This shift towards entrepreneurship was also influenced by her role at the Queensland University of Technology, where she facilitated mandatory Cultural Competence training for university staff, further solidifying her expertise in the field.

Building BlackCard

Mundanara's entrepreneurial journey was shaped by the wisdom and resilience of her family. She fondly recalls the influence of her grandmother, who instilled in her a deep sense of cultural pride and taught her Aboriginal versions of nursery rhymes. Her grandmother was a prominent Aboriginal figure who played a pivotal role in the establishment of Aboriginal community initiatives, including Radio Redfern and the first Aboriginal dance theatre in Redfern.

Mundanara's business acumen was further honed through her work with various organizations, both Aboriginal and mainstream. It was through her mentorship from Dr. Lilla Watson, one of the first Aboriginal academics at the University of Queensland, that Mundanara was invited to co-found BlackCard with Dr. Watson, Dr. Mary Graham, and her great uncle, Charlie Watson. BlackCard grew out of university-level courses on cultural competence, developed by respected Indigenous academics. The early years of the business were financially difficult, and Mundanara relied on her aunt's personal credit card to cover the costs of setting up the website, legal fees, and other expenses.

Challenges and Growth

The early years of BlackCard were fraught with challenges. Mundanara recalls a $60,000 debt in the second year of operations and the constant pressure to wrap up the business. Despite the financial struggles and advice to abandon the venture, she persisted, driven by her vision and commitment to the work. She supplemented her income with part-time jobs to manage her finances, but it was a major breakthrough when the Commonwealth Bank approached BlackCard to develop a cultural capability framework. This partnership marked the turning point for the business, leading to further successful contracts and partnerships.

Mundanara's journey as a businesswoman is also reflected in her decision to pursue higher education. Despite the perceived barriers, she enrolled in the MBA program in Indigenous Business Leadership at Monash University, which was co-designed by Aboriginal and Torres Strait Islander communities. Managing her studies while balancing work and family was demanding, but she found that the program reignited her passion for learning, particularly in Indigenous business and leadership models.

Policy and Recommendations

Drawing from her experiences in government and her personal journey, Mundanara advocates for systemic change in education and support for Indigenous business. She recommends introducing entrepreneurship courses in high schools, particularly in remote communities, to equip young Indigenous people with the skills and knowledge to succeed in business. She believes it is crucial for the curriculum to include the history of Aboriginal trade systems, emphasizing that Indigenous peoples have a rich history of governance and sustainable business practices that can inspire future generations.

Mundanara is also vocal about the need for greater transparency in government funding for Aboriginal community-controlled organizations. She stresses the importance of including Indigenous voices in decision-making processes to address the deep disparities faced by Aboriginal peoples, particularly in education and employment opportunities. "An Aboriginal child is more likely to end up in prison than to finish their final years of high school," she notes, highlighting the urgency of addressing these issues early in a child's life.

Conclusion

Mundanara Bayles has followed in the footsteps of her ancestors, advocating for Aboriginal rights and leading with resilience and determination. Through her work with BlackCard, she has made significant strides in promoting cultural competence and understanding across various sectors, contributing to the broader goal of reconciliation and healing. Her story serves as a powerful example of how, despite the challenges posed by intergenerational trauma and systemic inequality, Indigenous Australians continue to demonstrate remarkable strength, resistance, and a commitment to building a better future. Through initiatives like BlackCard, Mundanara is fostering a deeper understanding of Aboriginal culture and history, paving the way for greater inclusivity and a more just society.

Bibliography

Delgado, R., & Stefancic, J. (2001). *Critical Race Theory: An Introduction*. NYU Press. www.jstor.org/stable/j.ctt9qg26k

Denzin, N., Lincoln, Y., & Smith, L. (2008). *Handbook of Critical and Indigenous Methodologies*. https://doi.org/10.4135/9781483385686

Fairlie, R. W., & Fossen, F. M. (2020). Defining Opportunity versus Necessity Entrepreneurship: Two Components of Business Creation. In S. W. Polachek & K. Tatsiramos (Eds.), *Change at Home, in the Labor Market, and On the Job* (Vol. 48, pp. 253–289). Emerald Publishing Limited. https://doi.org/10.1108/S0147-912120200000048008

Guenther, J., Osborne, S., Arnott, A., & McRae-Williams, E. (2017). Hearing the voice of remote Aboriginal and Torres Strait Islander training stakeholders using research methodologies and theoretical frames of reference. *Race Ethnicity and Education*, *20*(2), 197–208. https://doi.org/10.1080/13613324.2015.1110294

Menzies, K. (2019). Understanding the Australian Aboriginal experience of collective, historical and intergenerational trauma. *International Social Work*, *62*(6), 1522–1534. https://doi.org/10.1177/0020872819870585

Morley, S. (2014). *Success Factors for Indigenous Entrepreneurs and Community-based Enterprises.* Closing the Gap Clearinghouse. Retrieved 1st March 2024 from https://apo.org.au/sites/default/files/resource-files/2014-04/apo-nid39458.pdf

O'Loughlin, M. (2009). A psychoanalytic exploration of collective trauma among indigenous Australians and a suggestion for intervention. *Australasian Psychiatry*, *17*(1_suppl), S33–S36. https://doi.org/10.1080/10398560902948746

Vivian, A., & Halloran, M. J. (2022). Dynamics of the policy environment and trauma in relations between Aboriginal and Torres Strait Islander peoples and the settler-colonial state. *Critical Social Policy*, *42*(4), 626–647. https://doi.org/10.1177/02610183211065701

Vivian, A., Jorgensen M, & Reilly A. (2018). Indigenous self-government in theAustralian Federation. *Australian Indigenous Law Review*, *20*, 215–242.

World Health Organization. (2022). *Social determinants of health.* Retrieved 01/06/2023 from www.who.int/health-topics/social-determinants-of-health

3 Jenifer Darr: Supporting Present and Future Indigenous Entrepreneurs

https://jadeeconsulting.com.au/services/

Meena Chavan, Jane Menzies, and Leanne Holt

Introduction

Jadee Consulting delivers holistic strategic services that develop frameworks and architecture to ensure that community development outcomes are achieved through genuine ownership and leadership, driven by the principles of self-determination to promote robust levels of self-governance.

They harness their combined organisation tools to build process and procedure design, change management, land conservation management and community development expertise, tailoring our services to suit long-term aspirations.

They have a deep knowledge of community issues, Native Title and community management frameworks that enables us to partner with and advise clients from across the community, private sector and government on the design, implementation, and monitoring of tailored solutions in Indigenous affairs, diversity and inclusion.

They work directly with the community to enshrine strategic and measurable approaches to achieve transformative community change.

Fostering the growth of Aboriginal Controlled Community Health Services (ACCHSs) is a vital measure in enhancing confidence, success and overall wellness within Aboriginal and Torres Strait Islander communities (Pearson et al., 2020). Since the establishment of the first ACCHS in Redfern in 1972, the industry has grown to more than 145 health organisations nationally (Darr et al., 2021). The community-guided approach of ACCHSs ensures members of regional and remote areas can access adequate and culturally competent care. The utilisation of ACCHSs is an initiative that aims to achieve the goals outlined by the 2020 Closing the Gap Report (Department of Prime Minister and Cabinet, 2019), and to address the disproportionate rates of negative health outcomes among Indigenous Australians when compared with non-Indigenous Australians (Australian Institute of Health and Welfare, 2022; Darr et al., 2021). Although there are numerous advantages to ACCHSs, navigating the complex accreditation processes can pose difficulty for Indigenous entrepreneurs wanting to provide support to

DOI: 10.4324/9781003386230-3

their communities. This chapter will review the importance of community-led support and initiatives and the opportunities for policy to assist in this growing space.

Working within the health industry for more than two decades, Jenifer Darr has a wealth of knowledge from which to draw upon when faced with the accreditation hurdles that come with entrepreneurship, particularly in the medical and health space. She has over 25 years of experience in delivering reform and change management. With a professional background in nursing, management, compliance and governance, Indigenous health, and public health, she is committed to the principle of reciprocity serving the Indigenous Australian community.

Early Life and Heritage

Jenifer has Aboriginal heritage from her father and Vanuatu heritage on her Mother's side. She is a Yuwi Vanuatu woman and comes from a chiefly line. Of this, Jenifer states, *"I feel very blessed and I am proud of my heritage."* Her mother's parents were removed from their homeland of the then New Hebrides (now Vanuatu) as slave labour for the Australian sugar cane industry. An Australian government sanctioned policy, Jenifer's maternal parents came to Australia as part of the slave trade (indentured labour) and the human labour force to grow the Australian sugar industry. Of the importance of her Aboriginal heritage and its influence on her business ideology, Jenifer states, *"Aboriginal people have always been here, for 65 millennia, and we've traded in that whole entire time"*.

In the 1950s, her parents, family and other Aboriginal, Vanuatu and Torres Strait community members built a church where these community members could go and worship. *"My parents were Christians, and their faith was unwavering".* The community church was built in a time when Aboriginal people in Australia were not considered human. (Strelein & Dodson, 2001) (FYI, the 1967 referendum removed references in the Australian Constitution that discriminated against Aboriginal and Torres Strait Islander people, Section 127 & words from s51 (xxvi – to remove () section after consideration).) In the 1970s, her parents and other family members started working on establishing a local housing business which contributed immensely to the community as there was limited access to rental property in the area at the time. Jenifer recalls, *"that started in the 1970s and I can proudly say it's still going today and it's the biggest real estate in the Burdekin area."* She credits her success to the legacy of her family and their Christian values. *"I am here today because of all of them."* Jenifer's parents' entrepreneurial journey added to the housing business when they diversified the business by buying a tomato farm. Growing up, she had to work on the farms. However, she was sacked from the job by her mother after she saw Jenifer disagreeing with the manager. *"My parents said to me either find a job in the next two weeks or go back to high school."*

Education

Jenifer went to a local public school near her home. She lived in a multicultural locality which she notes had a substantial impact on her upbringing. *"I'm so thankful that I was raised in that environment because we had neighbours who were Spanish, Italian, and Yugoslav. It was just this melting pot of different kids."*

She then decided to pursue a career in nursing across various areas for 21 years and got tired of the shift work and became more interested in management. She enrolled herself in a Master of Public Health and Tropical Medicine from James Cook University in 1997 and a Master of Business Administration. These degrees played an instrumental role in developing the business acumen that has allowed her to apply the learnings in the practical world. Jenifer is currently pursuing her Ph.D. in Health Systems Strengthening from James Cook University.

How did the Business start?

In 2018, she was in Victoria and lost her job which led to her contemplating starting a business. *"I'm like what am I gonna do, what am I gonna do, I mean I am religious and so I just thought what I can do in my business?"* That December, she registered her business and started advertising the following month. However, it was not until the following July that she got her first contract. That contract was walking beside a remote business going through first time accreditation for their three-year accreditation cycle which she has been working on until recently.

She offers community-controlled services to organisations based in remote areas that lack understanding and skillsets related to the various certification and accreditation processes. She excels in nurturing NGOs to navigate their certification and accreditation process. She also changed her business model to also cater to the capacity building of organisations and individuals. *"Here I actually want to be able to give them some level of skill to be able to navigate accreditation and accreditation standards."*

Jenifer's business has a stable demand as it services a closed community of 1000 people who aim to grow their skill sets and managerial capabilities in order to navigate complex accreditation processes. Her focus has been on training and upskilling staff so that they can provide services to their clients. Jenifer has delivered *"a number of Zoom education sessions with staff to be able to give them the skills, because what I needed them to do is read the standard then be able to interpret the standard and apply it to the service environment."*

She aims to be more than a paid consultant to clients. Most consultants are solely focused on the accreditation process and getting done with it. However, Jenifer aims to build capacity. *"If they actually just paid consultants to come to do that and then go, next time you have to get another consultant in to do the same thing which is leaving no capacity or building the education support required within the business."*

The business is still in its introductory stage and continues to grow. Most of the clients Jenifer is getting are from the referrals of existing clients. Another aspect of the business is the support that she provides in the Native Title process. *"Native Title custodianship of our Country handed back our unceded land and seas to manage our cultural heritage. The issue for us is that for every state in Australia they've got different state by state cultural heritage laws which doesn't make it easy, and the Native Title legislation is federal legislation."* Two separate pieces of legislation to comply with to leverage off and benefit from our allodial title.

Jenifer is committed to improving the community through her business and believes that she can bring about positive outcomes for her people. *"It's about capacity building for everybody else and then to change the dynamics of a community to be able to say; with this we can collectively do better."*

She is focusing her efforts on establishing the business in Australia first and then moving internationally. *"If we can make it work there when we can make it work in other locations because it's about setting up co-design and co-production through a community development framework."*

She believes that she can replicate the same model with modifications in foreign countries. *"In foreign countries, it's about having a model where you train and capacity build people and organisations in the foreign countries for job opportunities, there is a huge opportunity in the Asia Pacific region as well."*

Challenges

As Jenifer has worked for 25 years in the community-controlled health service sector, she understands the nuances of the accreditation process. However, she thinks that although the network and experience were helpful for her in establishing the business many unanticipated challenges arose. Jenifer remarks that it was *"probably a bit naive on my behalf that it would be easy."*

It was soon after registering the business that she found she was unable to generate clients despite her existing network within the industry. She also had to navigate the lockdown when most businesses were shutting down. *"I thought how do I do this?"*. However, she utilised her network with contacts from other industries and that provided her the support and confidence needed to stay in business.

Recommendations for Government

Jenifer has also used her knowledge of the ACCHS accreditation process to aid research and literature in the space. In a literature review of the efficiency and sustainability in the ACCHS sector, Jenifer and colleagues reviewed the effectiveness of having multiple accreditation standards for ACCHSs to enforce. The review found that the cost, time, and complexity of the processes were likely hindering service providers, however she also included many suggestions for government and accreditation bodies, such as addressing "issues of participation, governance and the politics of power, decision making and empowerment" (Darr et al., 2021).

Jenifer believes that there is a need for the community to have more role models as entrepreneurs. *"We need lots of Indigenous people to start businesses to show them the pathway and be the forerunners to them."* Jenifer believes that the government has to play an active role in supporting Aboriginal businesses. She does not want to pinpoint any one element of the government that has held back the community from entering and excelling in the businesses. *"I can't put my finger on what it was or what can the government do to help with this."*

Jenifer organically grew her network through her long history of working within the healthcare industry, which allowed her to overcome tough phases. However, there were no formal network opportunities provided by the government or any other agency. *"I didn't get any support at the national level. I suppose for me as a solo person running this business, probably was a blessing in disguise because I knew it was only me."* However, she considers that for future entrepreneurs, such support could be extremely beneficial. *"It will help in some ways, you try and do something, but it equally requires concerted effort from government"* The socio-economic determinants of health for Indigenous entrepreneurs must come into sharp focus for local, state, and federal governments in Australia. The effects of colonisation as an economic determinant have thwarted our business efforts. One solid measure is the targeted support of 100% owned Indigenous companies if the federal government seeks to see the chasm in the current 'close the gap' measures radically achieved. Globally, we are the longest continuous culture, 65 millennia identifies our measures of resilience as First Nation peoples. *"We know, understand and value the business of trade and commerce with its affect, impact and influence felt community wide."*

Conclusion

Jenifer's entrepreneurial drive can in many ways be attributed to her upbringing and the work ethic instilled in her by her parents. She notes, "*it's their legacy and Christian beliefs that they instilled in me that actually keeps me going.*"

Foley and Hunter (2013) highlight that historically, the term "Business" has been used to describe "customary forms of ceremony, ritual and kinship among family members" when used in the Indigenous context. The importance of kinship and family in Aboriginal communities has been widely noted as a cornerstone of Indigenous identity. Although, Evans and Williamson (2017) highlight that there is a "central tension" at play in Indigenous entrepreneurship, in which success is measured by colonial standards, Pearce (2017) states, entrepreneurship becomes an "act of both resistance to, and resilience from colonization."

Not only colonization, but ongoing policy has forced many Indigenous families to be separated, which creates intergenerational impacts on the social fabric of both individuals and communities. Therefore, the empowerment of family and community is central to the driving force behind many Indigenous entrepreneurs (Pearce, 2017; Shirodkar & Hunter, 2019) as it can be seen as a response to these policies, but also as a means of survival and self-sufficiency. Evans and Williamson (2017) state that the "collectivist motivations" upheld by Indigenous entrepreneurs (including family, role modelling, contribution to community and "emphasis on the relational and cultural strengths of entrepreneurship") are part of what makes Indigenous entrepreneurs so driven to succeed.

When these factors are understood in the context of Jenifer's story, it highlights the invaluable lessons learned by watching her parents use entrepreneurship as way to strengthen their community. Jenifer's passion for supporting other Indigenous Australian entrepreneurs is underpinned by her desire to help her community and foster the empowerment of the next generations in the same way her parents did for her.

Jenifer has made a tangible impact within her community by helping businesses and supporting others in growing their businesses. She is a highly organised person who does not take on any work if she does not have the competence in it. She is also very resilient and has a lot of empathy for the community. It is her drive to provide a better future for the community that keeps her going.

References

Australian Institute of Health and Welfare. (2022). *Indigenous health and wellbeing*. Retrieved 02/06/2023 from www.aihw.gov.au/reports/australias-health/indigenous-health-and-wellbeing

Darr, J., Franklin, R., McBain-Rigg, K., Larkins, S., Roe, Y., Panaretto, K., Saunders, V., & Crowe, V. (2021). Quality management systems in Aboriginal Community Controlled Health Services: a review of the literature. *BMJ Open Quality*, *10*(3), e001091. https://doi.org/10.1136/bmjoq-2020-001091

Department of Prime Minister and Cabinet. (2019). *Closing the Gap: Prime Minister's Report 2020*. Retrieved 02/06/2023 from www.pmc.gov.au/news-centre/indigenous-affairs/closing-gap-2019-report

Evans, M., & Williamson, I. (2017). Indigenous Entrepreneurial Motivations: Purpose, Profit and Leadership. *Journal of Australian Indigenous Issues*, *20*(1), 6–22. https://doi.org/10.3316/informit.149231485433376

Foley, D., & Hunter, B. (2013). What is an Indigenous Australian business? . *Australian Journal of Indigenous Issues*, *16*(3), 66–74.

Pearce, S. (2017). Contextualising female Indigenous entrepreneurs in Australia: Historical features of economic development and entrepreneurship in indigenous Australia. *Journal of Australian Indigenous Issues*, *20*(1), 41–56.

Pearson, O., Schwartzkopff, K., Dawson, A., Hagger, C., Karagi, A., Davy, C., Brown, A., Braunack-Mayer, A., on behalf of the Leadership Group guiding the Centre for Research Excellence in Aboriginal Chronic Disease Knowledge, T., & Exchange. (2020). Aboriginal community controlled health organisations address health equity through action on the social determinants of health of Aboriginal and Torres Strait Islander peoples in Australia. *BMC Public Health*, *20*(1), 1859. https://doi.org/10.1186/s12889-020-09943-4

Shirodkar, S., & Hunter, B. (2019). Factors underlying the likelihood of being in business for Indigenous and non-Indigenous Australians. *Australian Journal of Labour Economics, 22*(1), 5–28. https://doi.org/10.3316/ielapa.017682708350484

Strelein, L., & Dodson, M. (2001). Australia's Nation-Building: Renegotiating the Relationship between Indigenous peoples and the State. *The University of New South Wales Law Journal*, 24(3), 826–839.

4 Nicole Monks: Having a Social Impact through Art

https://wearebrave.au/portfolio/black-and-white-creative/

Meena Chavan, Jane Menzies, and Leanne Holt

Human Centred Design led strategies to build stronger and more capable businesses.

At Brave, we believe that to build a strong and remarkable business, people need to be the central focus across all things you do.

Black and White Creative creates opportunities for cross-cultural collaboration and more specifically, aims to raise awareness around the significance of our indigenous past, its relevance to our present and to ensure it has a place in our future.

They are a strategic design and business consultancy focused on developing customer-aligned strategies that drive growth and new opportunities for our clients. They use human-centred design strategies to uncover insights into the needs of a client's customers using strategic positioning and storytelling to drive engagement and impact. They believe that the strongest businesses are those that know who they are, understand their purpose and the value they are delivering for their customers.

Introduction

Nicole Monks is an award-winning artist and designer of Aboriginal Yamaji Wajarri, Dutch, and English heritage. As a multidisciplinary creative, she brings a conceptual approach to her work, weaving together storytelling that connects the past with the present and future. Through her designs, Nicole incorporates Aboriginal philosophies of collaboration, innovation, and sustainability across various contemporary art forms.

Nicole is the director of **Black and White Creative**, a cross-cultural design company focused on sustainability and regenerating local communities through art and cultural unity. She is also the founder and director of **mili mili Pty Ltd**, an Aboriginal public art company. In addition to her leadership roles, Nicole advises on several boards and committees, all while creating her own artistic and design projects that highlight Indigenous narratives and sustainability

DOI: 10.4324/9781003386230-4

Early Years

Born on Noongar Country in Western Australia, Nicole's early childhood was spent in the small surfing town of Pacific Palms, New South Wales. Her father, a builder, and her mother, a nurse with a passion for home design, instilled in her an appreciation for the built environment. Nicole recalls her childhood, saying:

"My dad was a builder, so we were always sort of building houses... I was the little mud mixer when I was about eight."

Her mother, though a nurse by profession, contributed significantly to the design of homes, crafting lead lights and creating beautiful gardens. Nicole's hands-on experience in these projects was formative, shaping her connection to design and construction.

Nicole grew up knowing about her Dutch and English heritage but was unaware of her Aboriginal roots until later in life. She explains,

"I grew up not knowing my Aboriginal heritage... it was a pretty interesting place to grow up because where I grew up, there was not much cultural diversity."

Her early passion for surfing saw her excel in bodyboarding, earning second place in Australia. However, after completing Year 12, Nicole faced a pivotal decision: to pursue a world tour for bodyboarding or accept a scholarship to study interior design in North Sydney. She chose the latter, marking the beginning of her design career.

Career Development

Nicole attended a private design college where she specialized in interior design. After nearly 15 years of working as an interior designer, Nicole shifted her focus to the built environment as a whole, developing a passion for how humans interact with their surroundings. Her formative years watching her parents design and build homes influenced her decision to specialize in this field.

It is admirable that Nicole was able to pursue her preferred choice of education. Indigenous Australians face significant challenges in accessing quality education, leading to disparities in educational outcomes compared to non-Indigenous populations (Menzies et al., 2024)As of 2021, the Year 12 or equivalent attainment rate for Indigenous Australians aged 20–24 was 68%, compared to 91% for non-Indigenous Australians, resulting in a 23 percentage point gap. Several factors contribute to this disparity. Geographical isolation, particularly in remote communities, limits access to educational resources and qualified teachers. Additionally, socio-economic disadvantages, including lower household incomes and higher unemployment rates, can impede educational engagement and attainment. Cultural differences and a lack of culturally appropriate curricula may also affect Indigenous students' connection to the education system (Menzies, 2004).

Efforts to address these challenges include the "Closing the Gap" initiative, which aims to reduce disparities in health, education, and economic opportunities between Indigenous and non-Indigenous Australians. While some progress has been made, such as an increase in Year 12 attainment rates among Indigenous Australians, the overall gap remains substantial.

While there have been improvements, significant barriers persist for Indigenous Australians in accessing quality education, necessitating continued targeted interventions and support to achieve equitable educational outcomes.

"I really enjoyed the process of thinking up an idea, putting it down on paper, and then building it in the real world," she reflects.

At 21, she became a senior interior designer at a boutique firm. She worked on retail projects and food outlets. However, by the fifth year, Nicole became disillusioned by the industry's unsustainable practices:

"Trends became very apparent to me... designs would be ripped out even when they weren't worn out. The décor was just a little dated, and it felt really unsustainable."

This realization led her to pivot away from corporate interior design, eventually establishing her own business.

Reconnecting with Aboriginal Heritage

As she ventured into entrepreneurship, Nicole began to reconnect with her Aboriginal heritage. She learned that her great-great-grandmother had been stolen during the Stolen Generations, a painful chapter in Australia's history.

"When I found out about that story, I felt a really deep connection," Nicole explains. "I really wanted to tell her story because she didn't have a voice."

Nicole's business became a platform for telling untold stories, particularly those of Indigenous people, like her great-great-grandmother. Her work focuses on creating spaces where Aboriginal voices can be heard, especially in the built environment, where Indigenous history has often been overlooked.

"The purpose of my business was just to help mob have a space to tell their stories within the built environment," she says. "Our mob has missed out on telling our own stories, and that's really important for me."

Her passion for telling these stories resonated in her projects, most notably a 3D mural commissioned by the Redfern Community Centre in Sydney. This project, designed to be eco-friendly, allowed Nicole to combine sustainability with Aboriginal storytelling.

Building the Business

Despite the challenges of maintaining a steady income, Nicole's business grew through her dedication to projects that resonated with her values. Her designs frequently incorporate Aboriginal elements, such as a chair inspired by the shape of a hunting boomerang, a piece that sparks conversations about deeper cultural meanings.

Her breakthrough came when she began collaborating with architectural firms that shared her values. These collaborations gave her the platform to integrate Aboriginal philosophy and storytelling into the built environment, which, in contrast to her previous work in retail design, had a lasting, meaningful impact.

"Some things unfold over a much longer period than just walking in doing a job at a Westfield," Nicole says. "For the relationship... there's no story, there's no nothing."

Nicole's projects often require significant personal investment, both in terms of time and finances. She reflects,

"You have to back yourself before you ask anyone else to back you."

Nicole's commitment to her work paid off, and with the support of a manufacturer, her designs were exhibited at a design expo. This led to her securing the first Aboriginal design grant from the Australian Design Centre.

Challenges and Policy Suggestions

Nicole acknowledges the challenges she faces as an Aboriginal artist in a field that has historically excluded Indigenous voices. One of the key issues is the lack of spaces where Aboriginal people can practice their culture. Nicole advocates for dedicated spaces in cities and councils for Aboriginal expression, such as unused walls in train stations that could be repurposed for Aboriginal art.

"There are no spaces available for Aboriginal people to practice culture," she states. "It's time that real things be put in place so people can practice their culture."

Additionally, Nicole emphasizes the need for government policies that allocate a percentage of employment for Aboriginal people in large-scale projects, suggesting that a "cultural fund" should be included in public art commissions to ensure proper engagement and cultural appropriateness.

Nicole also advocates for networking and community-building among Indigenous female entrepreneurs. She believes that mentorship and collaboration can help expand opportunities in the business world.

"We need to stick together," she says. "There's a lot of stuff happening, how can we do that? How can we make that work?"

Aboriginal artists in Australia encounter significant challenges in the design field, a domain historically dominated by non-Indigenous perspectives. The underrepresentation of Indigenous voices in design has led to a lack of cultural sensitivity and misinterpretations of Aboriginal art and symbols. For instance, the unauthorized reproduction of sacred designs on commercial products, such as the 1993–4 "carpets case," highlighted the exploitation of Indigenous intellectual property and underscored the need for cultural respect and legal protection. Moreover, the appropriation of Aboriginal art by non-Indigenous designers without proper consultation or understanding perpetuates colonial narratives and undermines the cultural significance of the artwork. This issue was exemplified in a 2023 incident where the National Gallery of Australia halted the promotion of an Aboriginal art exhibition due to concerns over authenticity and the involvement of non-Indigenous individuals in the creation of the artworks (Sheehan, 2011).

Additionally, the lack of Indigenous representation in design education and institutions limits opportunities for Aboriginal artists to influence design practices and ensures that their cultural perspectives are integrated into contemporary design discourse. This exclusion not only marginalizes Indigenous artists but also deprives the broader design community of rich, diverse cultural insights.

Addressing these challenges requires a concerted effort to include Aboriginal artists in design processes, respect cultural intellectual property rights, and promote education that values Indigenous perspectives. Such initiatives can lead to more inclusive and culturally sensitive design practices that honor the depth and diversity of Aboriginal art and culture.

Conclusion

Nicole Monks' creative journey is a testament to the power of connection—connection to her heritage, to the land, and to her community. Her ability to integrate Aboriginal philosophies into contemporary design serves not only as a platform for storytelling but also as a vehicle for cultural education. The significance of her work lies in its ability to bridge the gap between Indigenous and non-Indigenous Australia, fostering understanding and reconciliation.

Nicole's vision aligns with research by Kingsley et al. (2013), which explores the connection between Indigenous people's sense of belonging to country and their overall wellbeing. For Aboriginal people, a deep connection to the land is intertwined with cultural, spiritual, and social well-being. By using public art and design to tell Aboriginal stories, Nicole helps others connect to the land and culture in meaningful ways.

Furthermore, her advocacy for Indigenous female entrepreneurs echoes findings by Fang et al. (2022), who highlight that women entrepreneurs connected to strong support networks are more likely to succeed in their businesses. Nicole's dedication to building such a network through her company and mentorship opportunities exemplifies the positive impact of such communal efforts.

Her work continues to demonstrate that sustainability and cultural connection can be harmoniously integrated into the built environment, providing a powerful model for future generations.

References

Fang, S., Goh, C., Roberts, M., Xu, L. C., & Zeufack, A. (2022). Female entrepreneurs and productivity around the world: Rule of law, network, culture, and gender equality. *World Development, 154*, 105846. https://doi.org/10.1016/j.worlddev.2022.105846

Kingsley, J., Townsend, M., Henderson-Wilson, C., & Bolam, B. (2013). Developing an Exploratory Framework Linking Australian Aboriginal Peoples' Connection to Country and Concepts of Wellbeing. *International Journal of Environmental Research and Public Health, 10*(2), 678–698.

Menzies, J., Chavan, M., Jack, R., Scarparo, S., & Chirico, F. (2024). Australian indigenous female entrepreneurs: The role of adversity quotient. *Journal of Business Research, 175*, 1–14. Article 114558. https://doi.org/10.1016/j.jbusres.2024.114558

Sheehan, N. W. (2011). Indigenous knowledge and respectful design: An evidence-based approach. *Design Issues, 27*(4), 68–80. https://doi.org/10.1162/DESI_a_00106

https://www.closingthegap.gov.au/ Accessed on 23.6.23

5 Nicole Brown: A Female Leader of Indigenous Youth Entrepreneurship

www.dreamventure.com.au/nicole-brown-nicole-brown-consultants/

Meena Chavan, Jane Menzies, and Leanne Holt

Nicole Brown, a proud Larrakia woman, has broken down the Indigenous barriers through her Indigenous Engagement Consulting. Her passion to serve the community, along with her skills and knowledge, has transformed the lives and careers of many members of the Indigenous community. Nicole's accomplishments include being named Darwin's Citizen of the Year and Darwin's NAIDOC Volunteer of the Year in 2022. She draws upon her experience in the mining, health and community services sectors to support Indigenous engagement in the workforce.

She is a social activist whose primary aim is to advance Australia's First Nations peoples. Her diverse activities include investing in young leaders; facilitating safe spaces for people to come together; initiating purpose-led events; and speaking across the nation and the globe. As a strong single mum, she has a particular desire to support marginalised groups such as Indigenous girls and the wider Indigenous community. Her passionate advocacy and positive energy have been recognised through multiple awards including the 2022 City of Darwin Citizen of the Year and 2022 Darwin Community NAIDOC Volunteer of the Year. The thread connecting Nicole's initiatives is pride in her heritage and her desire to see her fellow First Australians thrive and prosper. By championing First Nations people and culture at every opportunity, Nicole is changing the narrative – and, ultimately, changing the future.

Early Life

Nicole Brown, as a child was extremely attached to her family, especially her grandmother. *"I was a shadow wherever she went."* Her parents were entrepreneurs who worked long hours to sustain their businesses. She learned many 'tricks of the trade' of business from them but she always wanted to do business differently. *"I wanted to work smarter, not harder. As a business owner, I want to be able to employ people to do that for me, so there is a method to my madness."*

DOI: 10.4324/9781003386230-5

Managing Business with a Job

Indigenous women in Australia face multifaceted challenges in securing full-time employment, deeply rooted in systemic barriers and historical disadvantages. Educational disparities significantly hinder employment opportunities; Indigenous women often have lower school attendance rates and educational attainment compared to non-Indigenous peers, leading to reduced employment prospects (Galperin et.al, 2021)

Additionally, institutional biases and discrimination persist in the workplace, with Indigenous women frequently encountering stereotypes and being pigeonholed into specific career paths.

Moreover, the scarcity of culturally safe and supportive workplaces exacerbates these challenges, as many Indigenous women report difficulties in finding employment that respects and integrates their cultural identities. Compounding these issues are limited childcare facilities, which disproportionately affect Indigenous women, making it challenging to balance family responsibilities with work commitments. These interconnected factors contribute to a persistent employment gap, underscoring the need for targeted policies and initiatives to address the unique challenges faced by Indigenous women in the Australian labor market.

Unlike her parents, Nicole was lucky to have kept a full-time job to maintain income continuity. Even now when the business has grown into something big, she is still managing to hold on to her full-time job along with her business and personal commitments. *"I've got a full-time job that really keeps me busy, which is good, and I just want to work on the fun stuff that I enjoy."*

Nicole does not compromise on any aspect of her life and gives proper time and effort to her job, business, community, and family. *"From Monday to Friday, 8:30 to 4:30, my head has to be in my full-time job. Then in the other waking hours, [I work on] my business. I try to put in an hour or two in the morning before my son gets up. If I schedule my meetings during my lunch breaks or after work and then at night time, I sometimes put in another hour."*

Nicole has been able to generate huge profits from the business, and as such, has to pay high rates of taxes for almost 40% of the income generated. *"I'm in the highest income bracket."* Despite the growth in the business, she does not desire to do it on a full-time basis. *"I've never looked at doing my business as a full-time job. I've really enjoyed the social aspect of being in full-time employment as well."* Having full-time work, has allowed her to be more selective in choosing her consultancy projects.

While there is a risk for burn-out, her commitment to the family and community is what keeps her going. Although she is occasionally pushed by others to expand the business into other areas she remains focused on her core area of expertise. *"[There are] cultural obligations for us as Indigenous people. Sometimes the lines get blurred and I felt like I was suffocating: people were trying to pull me in every direction possible."*

She receives queries and work requests from many different sources. In the past, large corporations have approached her directly to design action and education plans. A lot of work queries also come from LinkedIn where she has over 27,000 followers. The main focus of her work has been on the inclusion and reconciliation of the Indigenous community. Her focus is on educating allies. *"Educating them, it's not a box-ticking exercise, it's meaningful engagement."* She also believes in educating her peers *"my fellow Indigenous, First Nations people that are being proud of themselves and proud of their culture, finding their voices and actively using that, to the benefit of our* community."

Nicole has taken inspiration from Melbourne's "Code Changers" which helped her in understanding that there have been people and businesses that have addressed the same issues and there will be even more people in the future coming up with new ideas for the same issues. *"There are some amazing female entrepreneurs out there. They're just at the top of the game. They're breaking down biases, smashing glass ceilings, for the likes of me to come through in the next five to 10 years, so those role models definitely help."*

Gender Issues

She has faced numerous gender issues throughout her professional life. She reported that sometimes, *"I'm not being taken seriously. It's such a boys club."* She considers that many people in the professional world are not open to diversity and inclusion. *"I think we're always questioning accountability because we're so I guess risk-averse I don't know if it's just ingrained in us."*

She has faced many organizations that are apprehensive about her ideas because of the stereotypes. *"I have had in the past people telling me to stay in my lane and and I try to ring them or send them an email and they don't respond to them."*

Nicole has faced this both from large organizations but also people from within the Indigenous community have demonstrated such attitudes, even other Indigenous women have not been supportive of each other. *"There's a lot of lateral violence, and a lot of females attacking other females, which to me is just sad".* Furthermore, she indicated: "*Women in industry, we're not solid and we're not protective of one another, it is just laziness, and an opportunities for them to people to attack each other, I really don't like that."* Nicole though it would be better for everyone, "*if women to support each other and collectively fight the bias." "In the entrepreneurship space, be allies and have each other's backs, because you know, no, no one else has your back."*

Gender issues among Indigenous women in Australia are deeply intertwined with historical and contemporary forms of colonialism, racism, and gendered violence. Indigenous women face unique challenges stemming from the intersectionality of their identities as both women and First Nations people. They experience disproportionate rates of violence, including domestic violence and sexual assault, often exacerbated by systemic barriers in healthcare, justice, and social services (Cripps, 2016). Additionally, the erasure of Indigenous knowledge and culture, along with the dispossession of land, has disrupted traditional roles and practices that empowered women within their communities (Riggs, 2017). Indigenous women also contend with the marginalization and invisibility within both mainstream feminist and Indigenous movements, where their voices and struggles are often overlooked or misrepresented (McGuire, 2017). Despite these challenges, Indigenous women continue to play critical roles in advocating for social justice, cultural revitalization, and the protection of land and community (Behrendt, 2012).

Challenges

Nicole belonged to a family that had set a high bar for maintaining marriage; however, she could not continue with her relationship with her husband and that was extremely challenging for her, due to domestic violence. *"It was really exhausting process trying to leave and if he hadn't left, I didn't think I'd be alive today."*

However, she managed to turn her personal challenge around and transformed herself as a person by channelizing all that negative energy into something positive for the community. *"If you look in everything I stand for and what I do in my Community right now to what I was six years ago they're two different people. It's like I found myself. Probably through my son that he was the major driver."* She worked extremely hard because she had no other option but to fight. *"I actively worked three jobs to afford the lifestyle."*

Most of the challenges she faced in her business were related to taxation, however she managed to get in touch with the right people for advice. *"You always know someone will know, someone who knows, someone who could possibly get advice. So I feel that you know there's a lot more people out there now that are willing to give that advice."*

There are also a lot of networks provided by the accelerator program that has been launched by the government to support Indigenous businesses in Australia. *"There's all of these I feel networks out there, that if you don't have an answer for something you know where to find that."*

Learning from each other has helped Nicole, as she believes that she has been able to learn a lot in the process and has gained knowledge related to different aspects of the business. *"I feel that we've come in leaps and bounds again, it leaves my heart feeling good that it's progressing. We are progressing as individuals. Stakeholders and subject matter experts are open to collaborating more and sharing ideas more."*

Nicole has partnered with the Young Change Agents, who have a wide network across Australia. *"They will get the funding it's been funded to me, and then I pay subcontractors to deliver the training."* Nicole has been facilitating and managing projects and has subcontracted the training part. *"I picked up a group of facilitators to go and do it. I'll do the report at the end and collate everything, but because I work full time I don't have the time to go out and do it."*

However, when it comes to providing training to older women, she plays an active role in delivering the sessions on weekends. *"I can do it after hours or I can do it on the weekends doesn't affect my work, but then yeah I've picked up ladies who then subcontract to me to do this stuff within the schools. There's a school that is sort of close to my work, so if there are programs that are being run there, which is where I do frequently go."*

Expansion

Nicole is not yet contemplating expansion of the business due to personal and work commitments. *"Growth comes with additional stresses. I will potentially expand but it sits on the horizon for me at the moment. I'm enjoying where I am at."* She has a job that she enjoys doing and has a supportive workplace. In addition, she is in a growing industry, which has allowed her to get more job offers. *"I'm happy, I'm learning with a good work-life balance [there is] a good opportunity to grow."* Therefore, she has no current plans to leave her full-time job and focus solely on her business.

Being a single mother impacts greatly on her decision not to grow the business further. *"I don't have any extra hours in the day. I'm a single mum and I think any other hour that I have, I want to spend with my child."* Nicole enjoys taking her child along with her to different award functions and business trips, and does not consider motherhood as an obstacle or hindrance to her career. She sees entrepreneurial skills in her son, as well. *"The last time we went to the USA, we went over with an empty suitcase and came back with a suitcase full of toys so that he could sell them to his friends."*

Nicole is open to the possibility of moving abroad for some time. She had been involved in projects with the United Nations, and a move abroad may enhance her business prospects. However, she has no plans of leaving her hometown or staying abroad in the long run. *"I love my hometown. I want to see my hometown grow and prosper and people in it be happy. In the present, if I can play a role in that – that's sort of where I'm going to be."*

She has already chosen her sister as the person to look after the business when she decides to quit. *"I'm on succession planning, I'm looking to my sister to be the next me. She's come on board with me to learn what I do, and if in a year or two years she's comfortable, she may take my business full time."*

Recommendations for Entrepreneurs

For Nicole, it's all about making the most of all the opportunities. *"I feel like… take every opportunity that comes your way."* Even if there is something that seems difficult, Nicole believes that there are always answers to be found, whether that's through the Internet or by asking others. *"Ask other women, maybe in that space."* People at different entrepreneurial stages have varied networks and skills, and there is always a possibility of finding new and innovative answers. *"Build an ecosystem of about 10 other women in different career paths or as entrepreneurs."*

She believes that young female entrepreneurs should support each other, as she benefits from building such a support system around her. *"[There is a] sisterhood of amazing empowered strong women, either working in industries or working as an entrepreneur and you're just not afraid to ask questions."* Nicole is committed to supporting women from the Indigenous community by building a network of like-minded people. *"I can help you, I don't want anything from you, I just want you to be able to connect with the right people."*

Recommendations for Policy

Nicole thinks that the government needs to focus more on the education aspect from early on. *"I feel the government need to invest more in entrepreneurship education in mainstream schools."* She considers that entrepreneurship education can have a significant role in shaping the future of the country. *"I feel that as a nation we're going to thrive in the next 10 to 15 years on the back of entrepreneurship."* She emphasized many areas that are not considered mainstream but might emerge as key sources of growth; therefore, policymakers need to come up with ways to nurture the talent of the young generation. *"Looking at robotics, automation, and rocket ships, that people fly in every day."*

Nicole also believed that young people are more conscious of the community, environment, and sustainability issues. She referred to a conference she attended and mentioned *"there were 13-year-old girls talking about AI – how do we create apps so that it's safe for young women? There was another anti-bullying [app] so they're all thinking about ideas that they are facing. How do we find solutions to the problems that we are facing?"*

Conclusion

Nicole is a role model for all Indigenous, and non-Indigenous women who want to manage their professional and personal lives. She has created an extensive community engagement network throughout Darwin city. She is driven by her love for her people and is passionate about growing the next generation of Larrakia leaders.

Nicole's ability to balance the competing priorities of being an entrepreneur, a worker, and a mother is an incredible feat of time management and drive. As noted by Fang et al. (2022), many female sole-traders across the world note that personal and familial commitments are the number one source of friction in their career. The worldwide study showed that women-led organisations are at a disadvantage when compared to male-led businesses in this regard (Fang et al., 2022). As Nicole has suggested, creating networks of other women across industries may be a crucial method of providing support (in both a social and business sense) for emerging female entrepreneurs, helping them overcome the hurdles presented to them. Fang et al. (2022) also show that women-led businesses are at a larger disadvantage than male-led firms when personal networks are required, such as in the case of relying on trade or bank credit, or when there is low internet penetration in the industry. The study shows a quantifiable difference in the importance of having strong networks across men and women, as Nicole has identified.

Nicole's emphasis on fostering the next generation of young entrepreneurs is critical in developing a generation who are able to solve new and emerging challenges. As she noted, having a policy that addresses the educational structure has the ability to shape the future. Many children growing up today will work in industries that don't yet exist, thus, it is important to place the emphasis on transferrable skills, critical thinking and entrepreneurial ability that may help in future careers. As noted by a 2015 McKinsey Institute report on the impact of gender inequality in the workforce; women's minimized participation in the economy costs over $28 trillion in unrealized gains. Furthermore, the total gross GDP becomes capped at $108 trillion, where it could reach $136 trillion by 2025 should equal participation be able to be achieved (McKinsey & Company, 2015). Thus, the importance of encouraging the next generation of female entrepreneurs (particularly Indigenous women entrepreneurs) through early education is key to addressing the gaps in both social and financial economy.

References

Behrendt, L. (2012). Indigenous women's rights and gender equality in Australia: The continuing struggle. *Australian Feminist Studies, 27*(76), 125–140.

Cripps, K. (2016). Indigenous women and violence in Australia: Examining the link between colonization and social injustice. *Australian and New Zealand Journal of Criminology, 49*(1), 46–61.

Fang, S., Goh, C., Roberts, M., Xu, L. C., & Zeufack, A. (2022). Female entrepreneurs and productivity around the world: Rule of law, network, culture, and gender equality. *World Development, 154*. https://doi.org/10.1016/j.worlddev.2022.105846

Galperin, B. L., Chavan, M., & Muhidin, S. (2021). Indigenous Entrepreneurs in Australia: Past, Present, and Future. In J. C. Spee, A. McMurray, & M. McMillan (Eds.), *Clan and Tribal Perspectives on Social, Economic and Environmental Sustainability: Indigenous Stories from Around the Globe* (pp. 35–47). Emerald Insight. https://doi.org/10.1108/978-1-78973-365-520211006

McGuire, M. (2017). Indigenous feminism and activism: Voices from the Margins. *Australian Feminist Studies*, 32(96), 189–205.

McKinsey & Company. (2015). *The power of parity: How advancing women's equality can add $12 trillion to global growth. In McKinsey Global Institute*. Retrieved 06/03/2024 from www.mckinsey.com/~/media/mckinsey/industries/public%20and%20social%20sector/our%20insights/how%20advancing%20womens%20equality%20can%20add%2012%20trillion%20to%20global%20growth/mgi%20power%20of%20parity_full%20report_september%202015.pdf

Riggs, D. (2017). Re-claiming the Spirit of Aboriginal Women: Indigenous Women's Health and Wellbeing in Australia. *Australian Aboriginal Studies, 2017*(2), 22–33.

6 Kaylene Langford: A Creative Start-up Entrepreneur

www.startupcreative.com.au/

Meena Chavan, Jane Menzies, and Leanne Holt

Startup Creative is the place where risk-taking and creativity explode into action. a tool for entrepreneurs and future innovators, we equip goal-setters on their merry way to becoming colossal goal-getters.

Kaylene is a young Indigenous entrepreneur in her mid-30s. Inspired by her past experiences, Kaylene's business venture, StartUp Creative, aligns young, aspiring entrepreneurs with industry experts, development programs and incubation opportunities. StartUp Creative's focus on young people is crucial, as young people offer untapped entrepreneurial capital that will lead the next generation in economic growth. However, Gielnik et al. (2018) found that young people are less likely to transform their entrepreneurial intentions into actionable goals due to a lack of business experience. Developing entrepreneurial knowledge in young, Indigenous people is of particular importance, as the number of Indigenous-owned businesses is below the national average (Collins & Norman, 2018). This shortage stifles employment and economic outcomes for Indigenous people since Indigenous businesses are more likely to employ and reinvest in their communities than non-Indigenous businesses (Collins & Norman, 2018).

Kaylene supports and champions a new generation of Australian business owners and entrepreneurs who are willing to go the distance. With 10 years of extensive experience working with youth, Kaylene has mentored, developed, and supported hundreds of young people in achieving their dreams. Her business venture, StartUp Creative, has continued to evolve and expand with her team's dedicated efforts. Kaylene started her business in 2014 and has successfully run her business for the past ten years. Her desire to start her own business stemmed from wanting to step away from the corporate world where burnout and overworking were rife for her.

StartUp Creative provides a range of services for entrepreneurs and future innovators to progress their creative business ideas. The founder Kaylene, seeks to encourage risk-taking and creativity to equip goal-setters to achieve their dreams. Her services include a popular online platform, podcast, and print magazine that educates, inspires and supports creative entrepreneurs and

DOI: 10.4324/9781003386230-6

future innovators. Kaylene has over a decade of experience coaching, educating and supporting individuals to identify and achieve their goals. To supplement her business practice, Kaylene wrote her first book in 2021, on "How to Start a Side Hustle" which was published with Hardie Grant Books.

Early Life

Kaylene was born in North Queensland, with an Indigenous bloodline from her dad's side. Kaylene always felt a connection to the land and loved the natural spaces growing up on the Sunshine Coast, Queensland. However, she found out quite later in life of her Indigenous background: *"Mom started digging into it deeper than me, and she saw some family photos and had some conversations and, eventually, she managed to track down what our bloodline was and found that over the generations back on my dad's side one of the family members married an Indigenous women. So that was maybe about 12 years ago when my mom came out and said hey you kids are Indigenous."* For Kaylene, this helped connect the dots about her identity, and the past, and where she wanted to go in her life.

At a very young age, she went to work as a mentor for an Indigenous mentoring service which was an enriching experience for her. "*That was a beautiful experience in the Indigenous community there and working in a primary school. It was really nice to go up and be in that community."* It was her first engagement with the Indigenous community but that helped her in creating a deeper bond with herself and the community. It was there that she realized how much the community had gone through due to the treatment of Indigenous people over the centuries and the difficulties they have faced. *"The way that our Indigenous people have been treated is the reason why we're in this situation of taking so long to find out our bloodlines and feelings of shame around identifying it."* As Kaylene indicated, the treatment of Indigenous people, has meant that they have lost connection with their family bloodlines, and felt shame in doing so.

Kaylene describes her time working as a mentor in an Indigenous community as an enriching experience, suggesting the reciprocal benefits that mentorship can provide, as mentors often report newfound skills and confidence (Fredericks et al., 2021). Nevertheless, Kaylene also recalls the challenges and collective trauma that she witnessed the community face, which indicates the importance of having mentorship programs to enhance protective factors (Fredericks et al., 2021). When young people are provided with early support, the mentorship can have lasting, positive effects on the mentee in terms of social, health and educational outcomes (Fredericks et al., 2021). However, such programs are only effective in Indigenous spaces when mentors are equipped with the knowledge and training to be culturally safe (Sanchez et al., 2023). A systematic review by Sanchez et al. (2023) specifies that mentoring programs for Indigenous youth are more likely to be successful when they partner with the local community and focus on the strengths of the mentees.

Kaylene went to St. John's College in Queensland where she excelled in the sports excellence program, long-distance running and surfing came naturally to her and she took a keen interest in getting better at them. *"I just loved surfing and living near the beach, so I did what I needed to do."* She put in a lot of effort in track and field and was interested in joining a university that had a strong track program. *"I've been professionally running training from when I was 13, and by the time I hit 18 I joined the track team on the Sunshine Coast and was waiting to see if I was going to go to get into the State Championships."*

Kaylene recounts her passion for sports and aspiration to attend a track program at a university in the US, which points to the opportunities that sports can provide, as well as the personal meaning and support networks derived from sports (Williams et al., 2022).

However, there was an unfortunate injury that halted the progress of her athletic career. She then went to the University of the Sunshine Coast, but studying caused her a sense of confusion: *"I wasn't very good in science, it was mostly science and statistics and I did the first semester, and then about midway through the first semester, I was like I can't do this."* She soon got a job as an outdoor educator which was sort of an apprenticeship. *"I loved that job, and I went and worked in a camp and school camp. I started writing to my grandma who had worked for child safety, so I helped her design holiday programs for their kids in foster care. I just really loved designing programs and facilitating."* She also spent time volunteering for the Catholic Church in an Evangelization group for two years. *"In hindsight, it was there when I learned more facilitation and program development skills."*

She then got a job at School Chaplin initially and then at Marymount College which she did for four years. However, she was asked to leave that job because she decided to announce her sexuality of being gay and at that time it was not allowed. *"I'd have to quit or keep it a secret, so just I quit."* She then found another job and helped set up a new Flexi school. In this job, Kay worked with kids who were at risk because these kids were either drug addicts or kicked out of school for bad behaviour. *"In this job I helped kids who have been kicked out of school, or if they had become a drug addict, or if they were homeless or in and out of juvie, and my job was to help write programs for them and to help them learn and stay engaged in some level of schooling."* As Kaylene, indicated it was an unpredictable job while working with kids coming from traumatic backgrounds, however she felt she got a lot out of that job, as a result of helping others.

Subsequently, Kaylene's collective work experience exemplifies the importance of providing children with positive role models, as this can lead to flow-on effects for the wider community (Fredericks et al., 2021). For children who may lack role models and face hardships at school, having a mentor who views them differently can have a considerable impact (Fredericks et al., 2021). Furthermore, Locke (2022) emphasises that positioning Indigenous people as leaders is particularly imperative, as they have the nuanced knowledge and understanding to provide effective leadership in Indigenous communities.

After that Kaylene went to work for Queensland Council Social Service as a program officer where she had an opportunity to play her part in bringing reforms to the youth sector. *"We would advise the government on best practices, come up with policies, and then my job was to go out to Community and prepare them for new funding model to pitch for new funding models."* However, she was annoyed by the red-tapism and bureaucracy that was part of dealing with public projects.

As a program officer for the Queensland Council of Social Service, Kaylene experienced challenges due to the red tape within public projects, exemplifying research by Mex (2018), which found red tape to be one of the greatest barriers hindering grassroots leaders and volunteers.

How did Kaylene's Business Start?

When Kaylene was 24, she enrolled in a personal development course to try and figure out what she wanted to achieve in life. She then developed an interest in startups and entrepreneurship. Working with youth and being young herself gave her foresight that the next generation will want more autonomy. *"The next generation is just not going to jump on board with the nine to five, you know buy a house and settle down mentality, they want new opportunities, and challenges, they want to think outside the box."*

With that in mind, she came up with her business plan to launch Startup Creative. *"I wrote a program called 'how to turn your passion into a business' and I went and pitched it to the local council because I knew they had funding for young people and I got a couple of different Councils signed up."*

As Kaylene indicated, the business had started on a different track, but has now evolved into a much more comprehensive business plan. *"I just committed myself to learn everything I could about a business, so I started a magazine interviewing, successful business people, and then I would just try and interpret the advice in a creative and straight up way and develop programs. It's turned into a magazine, podcast and workshops."* Then councils also asked her to design programs. *"Hume City Council had me curate a startup festival, and then a bunch of masterclasses, which was great."*

Similarly, universities have also engaged her through various initiatives. *"Deakin University had me be involved in their Spark – Entrepreneurship Incubator program. I've done masterclasses for them and I've been on their panels for it, and as a judge for their student entrepreneurship competitions."* Furthermore, as Kay indicated, "*At Melbourne University, I went in and work with their entrepreneurship program and then separately I spoke at an event with General Assembly.*"

Kaylene has also been working for the LGBTQ community, for example she had conducted: *"Workshops with LGBTQ people in the workforce, and what that means and how to be more diverse. We also did workshops on Queer people in the community and how to feel safe in the workplace, and in the wider community, and to have allies and makes safe spaces."*

The business venture also provided consulting to independent businesses. *"There's been a few different businesses over the years. I was a finalist for the Telstra Business Awards, my magazine was in the Virgin Australia Lounges and I just got Wrangler on board, to do a professional meditation mindset talk to their staff at their professional development day."*

The use of social media has played an instrumental role in the growth of the business. *"In terms of Social Media, I got in early and I guess that kind of built our reputation."* The word-of-mouth was curated and that helped in building the business. *"People would share their articles which would give us a bigger reputation, because we had the knack of being able to get high profile people into our magazine."*

After working with youth, Kaylene envisaged that the next generation would value autonomy and flexibility in their careers. A literature review by Barhate and Dirani (2022) partially supports this foresight with its evaluation of Gen Z's job expectations as being inclusive of meaningful relationships, work-life balance, and stability.

Challenges

Kaylene experienced her first challenge, when she got an offer from someone from a startup company who had a similar business model to the one she was pursuing. *"We were kind of supporting each other to begin with, and then eventually it was like why don't you just not do StartUp Creative and come just work me and we'll just join forces and I was like no."* She took this as a positive sign as she considered that the person with such credentials did not want to compete with her.

It became difficult for her to manage everything on her own as she had to meet investors, and manage both operational and strategic issues. Her big break came when she met a *'big time'* investor in Sydney. As Kaylene said: *"I'd love an investor to just make this easier, so I can do the creative side but not have to hustle for the advertising. So I flew myself to Sydney and it was like the business floor of the Hilton. For a young woman, such business meetings can have challenges of their own. "I'm like this girl in her early 20s from the Gold Coast, and I got into this Hilton building that I would never step foot and it's just those two these two white middle-aged men sitting at this table. Apart from the receptionist, I am the only woman on the floor. They grilled me for like an hour. I was so intimidated."*

It wasn't about the content of the business meeting but how such meetings are conducted it can be daunting for a young woman, such as Kaylene. *"They're smashing numbers, which is fair, they're trying to understand if the business is viable, but it was going between two white men and I was trying to pretend as I fit in and I left the meeting and I walked outside and burst into tears."*

Following an intimidating experience with investors, Kaylene vowed to protect entrepreneurs by providing them with business training, as business-related skills are positively correlated to women's entrepreneurial success

(Welsh et al., 2021). Consolidating this notion, Efrat (2022) posits that interpersonal skills should be developed alongside professional skills, as they have become increasingly important in the business world over the past decade. Kaylene also recalls that it was intimidating being the only woman in the room, which mirrors the experiences of many women who are excluded from leadership roles due to the informal social networks of white, male leaders (Allemand et al., 2022). Hence, elevating the confidence of female entrepreneurs is imperative and Nate et al. (2022) suggest that startup support services much like Kaylene's can improve entrepreneurs' soft skills such as problem-solving and communication.

At that time she was new to such a male-oriented business environment, but with time, she overcame all the biases and came out stronger. She decided to do something about protecting young entrepreneurs from such challenges. *"My whole point of starting this business was to protect the creative entrepreneurs from the corporate white men who want to talk business at them."*

Finding the right people who support the idea and business can be tough because of the dearth of mentors around but she found a mentor who helped her overcome her fears and focus on the business. *"She was like you need to find people who believe in the dream that you're where you want to take it now, but you need to find people who believe in the way that you want to do it."*

Many of Kaylene's projects have assisted Indigenous people in developing their entrepreneurial skills and incubating their projects, which is crucial, as Collins and Norman (2018) contend that there is a shortage of policies and programs supporting Indigenous start-ups. Besides, Indigenous startups play key roles in sustaining Indigenous communities and improving employment opportunities (Collins & Norman, 2018). This suggests that it is important to have incubators to help support Indigenous entrepreneurial businesses.

The journey certainly has not been easy for Kaylene. *"It was really hard, it took me a while to get my confidence back up but there have been lots of little things along the way, battling making yourself a face of a brand and being inspirational."* In between all the business challenges, she also faced difficulties in her personal life. *"Going through breakups and leaving cities, and so like yeah probably the struggling life with being the face of an inspiring business is not always easy."*

Kaylene is looking forward to hosting two book launches this year. She is focused on expanding Indigenous communities through regular columns in newspapers and magazines. Many of the events have been canceled in the past two years because of COVID but she has grand aspirations for herself and the business. " *When we get back to the world of large events, being able to be in front of the noise, I've always been on stage and I really love being out there and doing that."* She is hopeful that soon she will be back in front of big crowds as the COVID restrictions are lifted. However, during the COVID-19 pandemic, she worked very hard on building an online community and has used social media to optimize the business. *"We've just built a network with an online platform and, yes, it growing and scaling."*

Although, Kaylene's business and mentoring services is not exclusively for the Indigenous community, most of her projects and work have helped the indigenous people. For example, *"Caroline runs Blak Wattle Coaching so she just got funding to do, I think it's a six-month mentoring program with Indigenous women in business and so she's asked me to be a mentor by the trainer."*

She was also asked by the General Assembly of Australia to speak on a panel for the global audience that was held in Chicago. *"I was a guest Australian Indigenous representative for that panel and we were all talking about the 'Black Lives Matter" movement and how people can be allies to black and other discriminated against groups."*

Besides all of the above activities, she has also been actively engaged in speaking to universities and helping students by mentoring them in making the transition to being a university student. *"I've spoken on their YouTube channel a few times and I get asked a lot to do it so whenever I get the chance."*

Recommendations for Indigenous Female Entrepreneurs

The first recommendation that she has to offer is to own your Indigenous identity. *"I am Indigenous and I'm proud about that, because it means that you get to set an example for other people out there who can grow and model your good behaviours. It is important to have Indigenous people in the limelight, who are doing something similar or aspirational to you, and then you know that they're also Indigenous, I think it helps you to think, that if they can do that, then I can do it too."* As Kaylene, indicates it is important to have Indigenous role models and leaders.

She also encourages female Indigenous entrepreneurs to break the stereotypes that are associated with Indigenous people. *"Change the narrative of what people have known as Indigenous people to be stereotyped as which is, as you know is not the greatest, which is we don't have an education and things like that so I think it's vital to put your name and your face, and your family behind it, to make it a better place in Australia for Indigenous people."*

From a business perspective, she believes that first, Indigenous Entrepreneurs must find what they love doing and then go all out to attain the business objectives. *"Don't be afraid to make money doing what you love, you know there's no shame in money and there's no shame in ambition being a leader, having a voice and standing up."*

Kaylene thought, that there was a lack of examples and role models in the community which often makes people a little reluctant when pushing the business forward. *"Sometimes there are people in the community, we don't want people to get too far ahead and that's you know, probably visibility shyness and shame in the Community."* However, she believes that with a clear vision one can overcome those hurdles. *"I think the more that we can stand in our power and do what we love and not be afraid to you know, provide for yourself and your family and find what you love and find a way to make money of it."* Kaylene encourages Indigenous females to find mentors and support groups that can push them towards their goals and provide assistance in difficult situations. *"Find those mentors and not be afraid to reach out and ask for help."*

Policy Recommendations

Kaylene thinks that the government needs to do a lot more to support the businesses from the beginning, by not only providing the funding but also building a network that can provide the support that is necessary to sustain a business. *"Because if this business isn't sustainable then you're not going to be around to be big role models so I think that mentors and coaches are needed and maybe some funding."*

Although she did not receive any funding from the government for her work, she believes that it made her work harder. *"I had to make a profit and I didn't get anything handed to me."* However, that made her journey a lot tougher, and to have more Indigenous female entrepreneurs coming forward, a lot needs to be done. *"Indigenous women need to catch up, there are so many things that set us back and confidence that needs to be built in those women. Putting them in the room, with other women who believe in them and I really do believe in seeing the role models and being in a safe space to ask for help and get mentorship or advice and some shortcuts. How to get in the game and stay in the game and do it well. I think that's game-changing."*

She considers that the government needs to create more networks and spaces for female Indigenous entrepreneurs where they can learn from the experiences and knowledge of others. *"That's what I'm trying to do with my community with my online Community it's like we can make that person that is I've got a space where you can post it here, and you know my mate will put on the beers or whatever, then that's the stuff that makes it easier. Having connections to help each other."*

Lessons Learned

Kaylene notes that governments should support businesses from their conception, not only through funding but also networking opportunities, as social capital is positively related to entrepreneurial success (Welsh et al., 2021). In particular, she argues that Indigenous female entrepreneurs require these networks and spaces to develop their entrepreneurial knowledge. This will lead to broader economic outcomes for Indigenous women, as Indigenous female entrepreneurs have a greater likelihood of employing Indigenous women than their non-Indigenous counterparts (Collins & Norman, 2018). Kaylene also mentions that allowing Indigenous women to learn from other women would improve their confidence and knowledge, as Nate et al. (2022) found that new entrepreneurs often lack belief in their abilities to act independently and to forecast their business.

Conclusions

Kaylene Langford is a young, strong and proud Indigenous woman, who despite all the personal and professional challenges has come a long way in running a successful business from which the general Australian and Indigenous community has benefited greatly. She is committed to driving the business forward and making an impact on society.

References

Allemand, I., Bédard, J., Brullebaut, B., & Deschênes, J. (2022). Role of old boys' networks and regulatory approaches in selection processes for female directors. *British Journal of Management*, *33*(2), 784–805. https://doi.org/https://doi.org/10.1111/1467-8551.12485

Barhate, B., & Dirani, K. M. (2022). Career aspirations of generation Z: A systematic literature review. *European Journal of Training and Development*, *46*(1/2), 139–157. https://doi.org/10.1108/EJTD-07-2020-0124

Collins, J., & Norman, H. (2018). Indigenous entrepreneurship and Indigenous employment in Australia *Journal of Australian Political Economy*, *82*, 149–170. www.ppesydney.net/content/uploads/2020/05/Indigenous-entrepreneurship-and-indigenous-employment-in-Australia.pdf

Efrat, A. (2022). Reviews of literature regarding interpersonal skills and the workplace over the years 2011–2021. *Network Intelligence Studies*, *X*(19), 53–63.

Fredericks, B., Daniels, C., Kinnear, S., & Mikecz, M. (2021). The mentor experience: Mentoring for Indigenous Australian school to university success. *Journal of Australian Indigenous Issues*, *24 (1-2)*.

Gielnik, M. M., Zacher, H., & Wang, M. (2018). Age in the entrepreneurial process: The role of future time perspective and prior entrepreneurial experience. *Journal of Applied Psychology*, *103*(10), 1067–1085. https://doi.org/10.1037/apl0000322

Locke, M. (2022). Asking the experts: Indigenous educators as leaders in early education and care settings in Australia. *The Australian Journal of Indigenous Education*, *51*(2). https://doi.org/10.55146/ajie.v51i2.12

Mex, C. (2018). Stepping up or stepping out? Recruitment and retention of volunteer leaders in grassroots associations [Journal Article]. *Third Sector Review*, *24*(1), 71–96. https://search.informit.org/doi/10.3316/informit.649929428492737

Nate, S., Grecu, V., Stavytskyy, A., & Kharlamova, G. (2022). Fostering entrepreneurial ecosystems through the stimulation and mentorship of New entrepreneurs. *Sustainability*, *14*, 7985. https://doi.org/10.3390/su14137985

Sanchez, J., Maiden, J., Barton, E., Walters, L., Quinn, D., Jones, N., Doyle, A. K., & Lim, D. (2023). Factors that sustain Indigenous youth mentoring programs: a qualitative systematic review. *BMC Public Health*, *23*(1), 429. https://doi.org/10.1186/s12889-023-15253-2

Welsh, D. H. B., Llanos-Contreras, O., Alonso-Dos-Santos, M., & Kaciak, E. (2021). How much do network support and managerial skills affect women's entrepreneurial success? The overlooked role of country economic development. *Entrepreneurship & Regional Development*, *33*(3–4), 287–308. https://doi.org/10.1080/08985626.2021.1872939

Williams, J., Pill, S., Evans, J., & Davies, M. (2022). ' … if my family didn't play football … we would literally have pretty much nothing': How high school Aboriginal students continue culture through rugby league and Australian football. *Sport, Education and Society*, *27*(1), 57–71. https://doi.org/10.1080/13573322.2020.1814716

7 Rebecca Wessels: Championing First Nations Culture through Art and Gifts

www.ochredawn.com.au/

Meena Chavan, Jane Menzies, and Leanne Holt

Rebecca Wessels, a proud Ngarrindjeri and Peramangk woman, is deeply committed to Australia's First Nations communities, storytelling, the preservation of language and culture, ethnicity, diversity, and multiculturalism. She is also the Chair of the Board of Ronald McDonald House South Australia, Board Member for Maxima Group and former Chair of Tandanya National Aboriginal Cultural Institute. She has combined her past corporate career and skills in IT and Community Services to build her business. Ochre Dawn is a 100% Aboriginal owned and managed operation, that strive to champion First Nations culture and art through partnering with First Nations artists to create artworks and products for commercial projects. The business operates through multiple channels, including Reconciliation Action Plan consulting, graphic design services, producing merchandise, corporate gifts, furniture, fitouts and providing training and consultation. Rebecca stands as the Founder and CEO, and states that she "*wants to live in a world where businesses prefer to partner than compete.*"

Early Years

Rebecca Wessels was born and raised in Adelaide's Kaurna Country. Wessels'mother was a nurse and she developed an interest in medicine as she grew up. Her father had entrepreneurial skills and started a business in partnership with a friend. When the business picked up, her mother left her nursing career to support the family business. As a result, Wessels gained some insights from an early age from the family business. She went to a private high school and performed well academically: *"I lovedmaths, sciences and languages."*

However, life was not always easy for Rebecca as her parents separated during her late teens. During her parents' separation, she did go a little off-track academically, dropping out of university twice. Wessels discovered her Aboriginal origin as a teenager. Interestingly, her mother got to know about her Aboriginal origins in her mid-30s, only when her biological sister came looking for her. Since Rebecca's mother was adopted, she did not know about

DOI: 10.4324/9781003386230-7

her origins. As a kid, Wessels was teased a lot for having darker skin, and later on in life she was finally able to realise why she had darker skin. Although Wessels knew about the Aboriginal origins it took her time to connect with the culture and family roots, as Rebecca said.

"It was probably over the next 20 years that it just then evolved into connecting with family, connecting with our culture."

It was not until her adulthood that she realized the impact her origins were going to have on her life. In her career, she had to tackle a lot of pre-conceived notions of people around her.

"The assumptions that sometimes are put upon you, in saying oh you're Aboriginal so, therefore you know, you can tell us about this food or this totem or this language and that, well I didn't get brought up with that, so I can't help you." Wessels has always been reluctant to share her story because she thinks that she's not an expert in culture. However, she realized that she can be of help to others by doing so.

Working Years

Wessels began her first full-time job in 1999 when she wanted a break from her family business and studies. The IT industry was booming at that time, and she accidentally fell into a good position, at the right time and place. She worked her way up in the next ten years and went on to manage a branch in her organization. She was 23 at that time and had to go out of her comfort zone to manage a branch with over $40 million turnover. Rebecca says she was "*managing a team of all men, mostly older than me, but it was a huge learning ground.*" The entire experience prepared her for all the challenges that were to come her way in her later years, especially giving her the confidence to run her business.

At the age of 26, she had a medical scare and at that time she was accelerating in her career and her medical scare had a substantial impact on her perspective on life. *"I didn't have kids or a husband, I always felt like I wanted to give back somehow and do some community service, so I did a lot of volunteer work and I was mentoring young former refugees andasylum seekers because I love the multicultural aspect and learning a lot of different language from them every day."*

She had to cut down her salary by three quarters by leaving IT and moving into Community Services, and during the processshe went back to the academic world to complete her Bachelor in Social Science. *"My mindset wasn't prepared for working in the community services space, and I needed more ...tools in my tool kit I think, so went back to full-time study, while working three jobs and then went into youth work."*

Building her Business

Wessels had the dream of having her own business and was driven to build a global empire. One day during her time in IT she was at Microsoft breakfast and started scribbling down business ideas on a napkin and she came up with the idea that community groups and businesses needed innovative and budget-friendly promotional products that could better share their messages. She had been introduced to such an industry in her childhood as she helped in her father's business where she developed an understanding of the supply chain for these products.

Rebecca ran her business as a side hustle during her careers in both IT and community servicesthen when she became pregnant she discussed with her husband regarding taking maternity leave from work and transitioning her side hustle to her full time gig. With encouragement from her husband, she was able to take that bold step in growing her business. Managing having children along with her business has been a challenge for almost 18 years.

"It has been amazing. As it grows I've just been thankful that it's still growing, even during the pandemic, this business has grown."

The business initially started as a promotional product business; however, there was a cash-flow issue that had an impact on the stability of the income generated from the business. Therefore, she took an event management role at Tandanya National Aboriginal Cultural Institute in Adelaide. The role allowed her to earn a separate stream of weekly income. However, she also got an opportunity to network with the artists who were working in the commercial space. She came up with another idea to seize the opportunity by connecting artists directly to the companies, governments, and universities that were sourcing First Nations art. The artists had difficulties in managing the license agreements, invoicing, and other related activities so this offer would be beneficial to them as well. This is when she came up with a business plan for a creative agency.

"In marketing you're storytelling for a business, the artist can tell the business' story through their art and the artist gets paid much more than they get paid at the local markets for their canvas."

Some of Rebecca's clients started demanding other services, such as graphic design, so she hired some First Nations graphic designers who could provide a cultural aspect to their branding strategies. Organically, the business expanded and it evolved from being a corporate gifts and promotional items company to a creative agency that now offers various services around the country. The artwork and culturally respectful services became the unique selling propositions of the service and helped in attaining a competitive advantage. The services they provided had a lot more to offer than just the First Nations design, but that became the identity of the service. However, the business has gone beyond that and now represents artists from a variety of backgrounds and styles. The clients have a much wider range of artists to choose from that suits their project.

"Sometimes we get pigeonholed into just doing the Aboriginal design stuff".

Wessels acknowledges the support that she has received over the years which has led to making the business so successful. For example, customers had acted as cheerleaders for them as many of their new clients are referred by them. In addition, Aboriginal friends have also supported her in the business by extending their network and support whenever it has been required. She also has had a couple of formal mentors over the years who have helped her with tactics and business.

Indigenous women entrepreneurs in Australia face unique challenges when starting and running businesses. Socio-economic disadvantages, including limited access to financial capital, hinder the success and sustainability of their ventures. Studies indicate that Indigenous women entrepreneurs often encounter barriers such as lack of business experience, education or training, racial discrimination, and lack of access to resources.

Additionally, many Indigenous women still experience a lack of cultural safety in Australian workplaces, entrepreneurial settings, and further education pathways due to ongoing encounters of racism and discrimination, and a lack of formal networking or mentoring systems. These challenges are intertwined with their identities as Indigenous women, making their entrepreneurial journeys particularly difficult.

Addressing these issues requires targeted support programs that promote resilience and provide the necessary resources to help these entrepreneurs thrive (Menzies et al., 2024).

Challenges

One of the major challenges that Rebecca had come across includes lateral violence, and mob attacks that came from different sources, whether it was other female or even male entrepreneurs. Some people thought Rebecca's business had exploited culture to make money. At other points in time, the business had encountered racism at times because of the services and products that they were offering. Furthermore, she did suffer a lot from stereotyping and incorrect assumptions that they were going to be expensive or couldn't do high volumes because it's a small business. However, this didn't occur all the time, and this business was very successful in what they were doing.

The clientele has been ever-increasing for the business, with some international clients getting on board as well. The business has been gaining some international experience as they have started directly importing from Europe, China, and India. Rebecca had gone to personally visit the factories in China and inspected for quality and other concerns. As Rebecca indicated: "*For our product sourcing, I like to make sure of the quality, as there can be terrible factories out there in the world, but also in our own backyard.*" By engaging in international sourcing, Rebecca, had also faced a lot of criticism for it because being an Aboriginal business, people expected her to make all the products in Australia. However, she has a clear idea of how to balance everything, "*Not everything is actually made here. You physically can't buy everything from Australia.*" In addition, Wessels understands the budget limitations, "*Obviously there's also the budget limitations, that the same product made here in Australia is often much more expensive."* Customers do claim that they are willing to pay more for Australian products, but Wessels sees nothing wrong in buying from overseas if it is done ethically, *" us First Nations people have traded with other countries, for many years."*

Much of the success of the organization is credited to the team and hiring plays an important role. Wessels focuses more on finding the right fit between the work, organization, and person. She believes that skills can be taught over time but if someone is not right for the role then it is hard to adjust. One other challenge, that was encountered by Rebecca, was *"Sometimes there is too much work available but not enough people because of the resource constraints so we have to let go of a few projects."* The business had faced many troughs and peaks, so it becomes hard to manage the human and financial resources.

Gender Issues

Initially, it was a challenge for Wessels to be the only woman in the room when she entered the business world. *"I worked for 10 years in IT, in very male-dominated organisations and it will often be that I was the only woman in the room and sometimes the company!"* However, she has now become quite comfortable working in a male-dominated setting. It becomes difficult when there is gender-oriented aggression and a clash of egos. Sometimes it becomes a challenge to manage negative situations in which it feels as if they (males) are being threatened by a woman in a dominant or successful position.

Not only men, but women can be a cause of the problem for Wessels, on occasion. *"During my time in the IT sector, some women felt the need to be competitive with others and would tear each other down. And in the First Nations business sector some other women-owned businesses have been attacked through lateral violence, or because someone else is successful."* Rebecca indicated that this could be because of jealousy, trauma, competition, fear or systemic barriers.

Recommendations

Wessels believed that the focus of budding entrepreneurs should be on developing a toolkit that encompasses skills, experiences, and qualifications. She also emphasized the importance of building a support network that can help them because it is a long journey: "*Make sure that you have a great cheer squad around you because there will be tough days, and it is quite a lonely journey being an entrepreneur as well."* Along with the support system, she encourages female led Indigenous businesses to find mentors who could provide guidance and coaching in related areas.

Another important piece of advice she offered was not to be afraid of failures: *"the biggest thing that I've had to learn, particularly being an over-achiever academic is to embrace and not be afraid of failure because it's inevitable you just have to."* The fear of failure does not allow people to go out of their comfort zones and once someone has gone through a tricky situation, that person may be able to learn something valuable in the process.

Policy Recommendations

Wessels emphasized that the government has to go beyond the paperwork and come up with practical steps for the betterment of the Indigenous people. *"They need to do more internally to move beyond the tick box exercise for things like the Indigenous Procurement Policy."* There also has to be a better attempt at focusing on community relationships with businesses. The government is using tick-box exercises for procurement contracts in which they select tiers of organizations in which they should be holding such companies accountable for the terms and conditions.

She has suggested that in terms of First Nations Women, the government should focus on developing and enhancing leadership capabilities. There has been a lot done related to the employment aspect but when it comes to board positions and leadership roles there should be more women represented at those levels. *"I think they know, we need to see more women at the board level and in senior management positions, but this is especially more important for First Nations Women because there is little to no representation of these women in the upper echelons of Australian organisations, and we should be actively advocating for First Nations Women to seek leadership positions."*

There has to be government support for the First Nations Women because they often undersell themselves because of stereotypes and the lack of opportunities. *"We always undersell ourselves as well, so I think actually when I say we need to be more – the government needs to be more – proactive in seeking and encouraging people into those women in those roles because most of the time we don't put ourselves forward".* Research by Fang et al. (2022) indicates that psychological traits such as "self-confidence, risk aversion, acceptance of competition and inter-personal skills" may attribute to workplace gender disparity. This notion, when met with the intersecting dynamic of Indigenous identity may have a substantial impact on Indigenous Women's advancement in the workplace and is a necessary area for future policy to address.

Conclusion

Rebecca Wessels has built a business that provides a unique offering to businesses. She has brought along with her all the IT and community service experience of her past and has integrated it into the business model in a highly successful manner. She takes pride in serving her clients as business partners. She has been a role model for First Nations Women as she has stayed true to her roots in her journey and has pursued her passion for preserving language and culture.

Rebecca's work in the Indigenous art space holds significant value, as the agency of Indigenous artists is critical to the well-being of the wider community.

According to the Office of the Registrar of Indigenous Corporations (2012), "art sales are the primary or only source of non-government income" among many remote and regional Indigenous communities. A draft report into Aboriginal and Torres Strait Islander visual arts and crafts by the Department of Prime Minister and Cabinet (2022) found that during the 2019–2020 period, a total of 19,000 Aboriginal and Torres Strait Islander peoples earned a total income of $26–37 million. The report highlighted that art centres sold around $5.1 million worth of souvenirs and merchandise, such as the type Rebecca's business produces.

The link between Rebecca's ability to synthesize her previous skills in management, and the burgeoning market for Indigenous art shows her innate entrepreneurial ability and awareness of the need for culturally competent businesses in the field. Art centre employees are noted as being pushed into "accidental entrepreneurs" (Seet et al., 2015) through the business structure, which typically involves a board of directors consisting of local Indigenous leaders (Seet et al., 2021). Seet et al. (2015) also note that this may be due to the requirement for employees to be "innovative and autonomous" to adapt to the steep learning curves around norms, rules and practices of the community, as well as the tendency for employees to be hired from outside the Indigenous art sector. Seet et al. (2021) recognise the multidimensional role of Indigenous art centres as they operate commercially (in selling Indigenous art), in the public sphere (in creating employment opportunities for Indigenous workers), and socially (through nurturing and developing young artists, and the continuity of traditional cultural practices). As Rebecca has detailed, her own experiences from IT to her current role have embodied this process of accidental entrepreneurship and have led to an organic and successful career trajectory.

Rebecca's utilization of a multimodal business approach is reflective of the innovation and entrepreneurial attitudes described above, and her diverse career history. Through taking advantage of her transferrable skills and personal development through her working life, Rebecca has created a strong foundation to build her business upon. Her experience as a woman in a male dominated field may have aided her in building the confidence necessary to overcome the psychological hurdles highlighted by Fang et al. (2022) above. Finally, Rebecca's desire to connect to her culture and provide support for other Indigenous businesspeople is foundational to her work.

References

Fang, S., Goh, C., Roberts, M., Xu, L. C., & Zeufack, A. (2022). Female entrepreneurs and productivity around the world: Rule of law, network, culture, and gender equality. *World Development*, *154*, 105846. https://doi.org/https://doi.org/10.1016/j.worlddev.2022.105846

Menzies, J., Chavan, M., Jack, R., Scarparo, S., & Chirico, F. (2024). Australian indigenous female entrepreneurs: The role of adversity quotient. *Journal of*

Business Research, *175*, 1–14. Article 114558. https://doi.org/10.1016/j.jbusres.2024.114558

Seet, P.-S., Jones, J., Acker, T., & Jogulu, U. (2021). Meaningful careers in social enterprises in remote Australia: Employment decisions among Australian Indigenous art centre workers. *The International Journal of Human Resource Management*, *32*(8), 1643–1684. https://doi.org/10.1080/09585192.2018.1528556

Seet, P. S., Jones, J., Acker, T., & Whittle, M. (2015). Shocks among managers of indigenous art centres in remote Australia. *Management Decision*, *53*(4), 763–785. https://doi.org/10.1108/MD-06-2014-0386

8 Carol Vale: Founder and Director of Murawin Pty Ltd

https://murawin.com.au/

Meena Chavan, Jane Menzies, and Leanne Holt

https://murawin.com.au/ Human Resource Consultancy
Murawin is a mission & values driven company that believes wholeheartedly in the work we do and it's positive impact on First Nations communities and the wider Australian population as well. Our mission is to create impact by breaking cycles of disadvantage and amplifying initiatives that contribute to improved futures for Indigenous Australians and other marginalised groups.

Carol Vale is a Dunghutti woman from Northern New South Wales and the founder of *Murawin Pty Ltd*, a leading national Indigenous consultancy firm. Drawing from her personal experiences growing up on an Aboriginal mission and an extensive career in the public sector, Carol is dedicated to improving outcomes for Indigenous Australians.

Murawin, named after the Dunghutti word for "to be educated," works with organizations to provide both technical expertise and cultural knowledge across a variety of social and public policy areas impacting Indigenous communities. These areas include Indigenous-led research, community engagement, and the integration of Indigenous perspectives, particularly the importance of *Country*, in policy development and execution.

Early Life and Influences

Carol's formative years were spent on an Aboriginal mission in Armidale, New South Wales, where she faced significant financial and social challenges. At 16, she left home and dropped out of school in Year 10 to support her family. Despite a deep passion for education, Carol's early life was shaped by intergenerational poverty, which hindered her ability to continue her schooling. This cycle of disadvantage, as identified by Baxter and Meyers (2016), often limits employment opportunities and perpetuates systemic poverty.

Carol later moved to Sydney, where she initially worked in a chocolate factory. Realizing it wasn't her calling, she returned to Armidale, completed a secretarial studies course, and secured a government job. She spent the next decade working in the public sector, building the skills and networks that would later support her entrepreneurial journey.

DOI: 10.4324/9781003386230-8

As the eldest of seven children, Carol often found herself taking on a leadership role in the family. One example of her resourcefulness and entrepreneurial spirit occurred when she and her sister wanted to go swimming but lacked the funds. "It wasn't just about us wanting to go to the pool, it was about us taking our cousins with us," Carol recalls. To raise the necessary money, they baked cakes and sold them for five cents to their extended family. This early experience aligns with research by Fairlie and Fossen (2020), which suggests that necessity often drives entrepreneurial behavior.

Carol's entrepreneurial instincts were further strengthened by her family values. "It was about coming together as a group and drawing on each other's areas of expertise," she says. "We would make cakes to sell and raise money for swimming." These efforts highlight the importance of community in Indigenous entrepreneurship, as identified by Peredo and McLean (2010), where family and community ties are central to business success.

Carol continues to integrate her family into her business. Several relatives work at *Murawin*, contributing their diverse skills to the organization. "My family members don't just get a job because they are family; it's about purpose fit," she explains. "They have the experience and qualifications needed to perform their roles effectively."

Her approach reflects the broader concept that Indigenous businesses, as Peredo and McLean (2013) argue, are embedded within community networks that offer mutual benefits. By employing family members, Carol ensures that *Murawin* strengthens its social fabric while providing economic opportunities to those who need it most.

Business Journey and Challenges

Murawin was established in 2014 after Carol transitioned from her government career to consulting. Initially, she relied on her networks, reaching out to Supply Nation members and the NSW Indigenous Chambers of Commerce. Carol began by offering cultural awareness training, later expanding into evaluation and research services. While successful, she acknowledges the difficulties of starting her own business.

"It was hard in the beginning," she admits. "We lived off my partner's wage and our savings. People knew me as a government employee but didn't know me as a consultant." Carol's experience exemplifies the challenges many entrepreneurs face when transitioning from public service to private consultancy. However, her adaptability and relationship-building skills allowed her to build a strong foundation.

Mentorship also played a crucial role in her success. "There was one mentor in particular, an Indigenous woman with ten years of consultancy experience, who helped guide me," she says. "She told me, 'If you can get through the first three years, you'll be okay.' And we did."

Her experience highlights the power of mentorship in building self-confidence and entrepreneurial resilience, as outlined by Nate et al. (2022).

Carol also emphasizes the importance of drawing on Indigenous networks and support systems in business, as these connections offer both practical advice and moral encouragement.

Overcoming Industry Barriers

Indigenous women in Australia encounter significant barriers when striving for managerial and leadership positions, primarily due to the intersection of systemic racism and gender inequality. This dual discrimination often results in Indigenous women being underrepresented in senior roles and overrepresented in lower-income brackets. Cultural differences between Indigenous leadership styles and mainstream corporate expectations can also pose challenges. Traditional Indigenous leadership often emphasizes communal decision-making and collective well-being, which may conflict with the individualistic and competitive nature of many organizational structures. Additionally, the scarcity of role models and mentors within corporate hierarchies can impede the professional development of Indigenous women, limiting their access to networks and opportunities essential for career advancement. Addressing these challenges requires a comprehensive approach that includes cultural competency training, mentorship programs, and organizational reforms to create inclusive environments that value diverse leadership styles (ABS, 2021; Dinku & Hunt, 2019).

Carol has faced considerable challenges in asserting her professional worth, particularly within mainstream corporate environments. One instance stands out where a corporate partner attempted to undercut her value. Despite her extensive experience, including a Master's degree focusing on intergenerational trauma and ten years of work in child protection, Carol was placed in a junior role within a team addressing Aboriginal child sexual assault.

"They thought I would do it for free because I'm Aboriginal," she recalls. "Yes, I want to help my community, but I also need to put food on my table." This experience illustrates the systemic undervaluation of Indigenous expertise and the expectations that Indigenous professionals should engage in "inclusivity" work without adequate compensation (Thunig & Jones, 2021).

Carol's response was firm: "I told them, 'If you want me to do the work, my rate is the same as yours.'" Despite the frustration, she remained professional, confident in her worth, and committed to her principles.

This situation is emblematic of broader challenges Indigenous professionals face, where their work is often devalued or dismissed (Lahn, 2018). Carol's determination to challenge these inequities mirrors the experiences of many Indigenous entrepreneurs and advocates who must constantly navigate and assert their professional value in a system that frequently marginalizes them.

Reflections on Growth and Empowerment

As *Murawin* has grown, Carol has become increasingly confident in her position as a business leader. "We've turned a corner," she says. "We now have returning clients, and we've built strong relationships with a dedicated team who understand and respect our work."

Carol's vision for the future is one of economic self-sufficiency and empowerment for her family and community. "It's not just about taking from a pay packet," she says. "It's about having enough income to choose where you want to live and what you want to do. I want to break the cycles of poverty in my family, so that they can access the resources they need to thrive."

Carol's commitment to empowering future generations is evident in her approach to her grandchildren. "We don't give them pocket money; we give them pieces of work. It's about instilling a mindset of income generation and wealth creation." Her desire to create lasting change for her family speaks to the broader issue of intergenerational wealth and opportunity for Indigenous communities.

"I want my grandchildren to have access to the services they need to stay happy and healthy, and to build lives of economic independence," she says.

Carol's story reflects the resilience, innovation, and community-centered values that are foundational to *Murawin* and to Indigenous entrepreneurship more broadly. Through her work, Carol continues to challenge perceptions and break down barriers for herself, her family, and her community.

Challenges of running a Human Resources agency "It was hard. We did a lot of work with the government, and we were sub-contracted out to a couple of organisations. We still have professional relationships with those few that gave us a go in the early days. They're the special ones that we never forget," she said. "I took on anything that came. It was just me and I did a lot of travel. I worked hard to build my reputation as a businesswoman." While Carol depicts the hardships of being a female entrepreneur, her experience is indicative of the resilience that is required in entrepreneurship, particularly due to gender-related and intersectional barriers relating to her Indigenous background (Shelton & Lugo, 2021). One of Carol's daughters now works at Murawin as their marketing manager. When they were just starting, she did their promotional material as one of her university projects. "We've come full circle with her," reflects Carol. "Fundamental to my business is about breaking cycles of poverty and creating mindsets around economic empowerment," said Carol. "That's why I'm excited that my three children are working with us, and then the other one has their own very successful business." "It is an opportune time right now because of the focus from both the Indigenous Procurement Policy (IPP) and the emergence of the Indigenous business sector. It is very collegial in a way. We understand each other and we have an opportunity to change the mindsets of our clients in the context of doing good and making an impact for Indigenous Australians." In addition to social entrepreneurship, Murawin runs the 'Morning Sky' project to give back to their community. Under its two arms, financial and economic empowerment, the project seeks to work with Indigenous women to empower them through work. "We do workshops about the power of business and the difference that business can make in their life." "We do a couple of programs with the

Commonwealth and State governments around bringing women into the conversation and helping them to understand that they can do business at whatever level they want to. It's about helping them to understand that they can do it in a way that fits with their lifestyle and needs." Carol reflects on a desire to increase the participation of Indigenous women in business through workshops which can improve their entrepreneurial skills and self-confidence (Nate et al., 2022). Additionally, Carol aims to demonstrate that entrepreneurship can be shaped around lifestyles, which corroborates Gherardi (2015) assertion that gendered notions of entrepreneurship and work-life balance should be reinterpreted as complementary practices. "We provide financial and in-kind support to a whole range of organisations that is about empowering indigenous girls and women," said Carol. "We're currently working with a couple of corporates around setting up a scholarship for an Indigenous girl to go to a boarding school. I always wanted to go to a boarding school to access that consistent education and never got to do it," she adds. Drawing on her past desires to access education, Carol supports initiatives to empower Indigenous girls and women through education. Such educational initiatives can improve the life outcomes of Indigenous Australians, specifically when engaging from a relational, Indigenous perspective (Keddie, 2013). "One of the things that we did very early on while we were setting up the business, was that we ran a national conference around tackling the impacts of child sexual abuse in our communities. The reason we did that is when I was with the government for the last 10 years of my career, I was working in the child protection area." Using their own money from the business, they ran a three-day national conference in Brisbane. "We wanted to get [tackling child sexual abuse] on the agenda – how do we support communities and the children impacted by child sexual abuse?" They wanted to approach the topic from a capacity-building position. "It was attended by some pretty high-profile people nationally and the network helps a lot," said Carol. "It's about the thinking that's required and it's the thought leadership that's required to support the continued growth and thriving of indigenous businesses," she continues. "I'm not seeing the research out there enough about that at the moment." "There's an emerging Indigenous business model and if you think about the current business models, they are constructed on the western values," she said. "Therefore, any measurements of success and any advice around how to do business is based on that thinking." Western business knowledges are often defined as overarching principles but may not be conducive to Indigenous success that derives meaning from values such as community, responsibility, and sustainability (Mrabure, 2019). Challenges "I'm very conscious that I want Murawin to be an Indigenous-led company. We are an Indigenous-owned company, and we will always be that" said Carol. "But I want my company to be able to work in the intercultural space. I want Indigenous and non-Indigenous people to be working for us at all levels. I want that grassroots communicator right through to the one that you can sit in any boardroom in this country." "We have that, and I want to grow that," she said. "One of the challenges that we still have is our new clients. Our recurring clients are starting to understand us and who we are. We don't have to keep educating them about 'Aboriginal 101'. "Cash flow is always an issue," said Carol. "Clients, big corporates take up to 90 days to pay. I know that that's their normal, and so that's fine, but we're a small company and they're asking us to carry them." "Getting staff and keeping staff is always a challenge as a small company but we've got a lot of systems in place now," she explains. "Accessing qualified mid-to-senior level Aboriginal people is always hard. They're either in their own businesses at the moment, or in good government or corporate jobs. Why would they come to a small Indigenous business?" asks Carol. "I'm trying to encourage others to come and take a secondment. That way, it's about building the competency of both our organisations and exchanging knowledge." When it comes to Indigenous-owned businesses, gaining access to loans from banks is challenging. "We haven't received any [loans], but we haven't gone to them," said Carol. "We've used our own money. We've got a grant from Indigenous Business Australia (IBA) and I would rather do that than go to the bank," she said. "We only did that once when Covid hit." "I've done that deliberately because I wanted to say that we did this ourselves." "We don't have the luxury of stuffing up," said Carol. "Because if we do, I feel as if my Indigenous business colleague sisters will be tarred with that. We can't afford to not get it right." "We have to go in there and if another provider provides a 100% service, we have to provide 160% to accommodate for the race stuff, and then the female stuff too." Carol mentions the extent the service quality is needed to counteract biases, which correlates with a study by (De Sante, 2013) demonstrating that implicit racism positions the work of minorities as less valuable than white people's work. Recommendations "We need to start early to get our children thinking about business and entrepreneurship," said Carol. "For instance, my daughter is working with another Indigenous business and her children are collecting seeds for this other business." They came up to Carol and said, "Nana, we made $80" "This is a five-year-old and a six-year-old and their mum has already set up an account for them," said Carol. "They've always come along to Murawin meetings, and I've got them doing small bits of work for me. I pay them and my daughter always says, 'Mum, I'm sure you're paying them way above the minimum wage' but it doesn't matter. I'm trying to break cycles of poverty." Carol aims to instill business knowledge and values in children early on, which can reduce cycles of poverty, as a literature review by (Silva-Laya et al., 2020) found that children who aspire for brighter futures can facilitate social mobility. "Murawin is a multi-million-dollar company now," said Carol. "It still just blows me away. I started Murawin by developing a product around what I know," she said. "As a public administrator, that was evaluation, research, and engagement with the community. Then I realised that there are a lot of people out there, other consultants, just as good as me." "Then I started to think like a business owner, reinventing myself and speaking the language of the sector. I had to quickly go and educate myself through books and attending programs to immerse myself in the sector." "I had to find an answer to the question, why me? It doesn't come easy for Aboriginal people, certainly not Aboriginal women. I had to stand up and make myself shine," said Carol. "That was hard to do in the beginning because I had to promote myself and speak about myself, but I had to do that." Carol recalls having to speak up and promote herself which is challenging as an Indigenous woman in entrepreneurship who faces greater obstacles in being recognised than non-Indigenous entrepreneurs (Lahn, 2018). Changing paradigms and perceptions "I had to think about money as a good thing. If you've got access to money and resources, that was about impact. I had to name the impact that we were doing. I had to say to my clients, "if you work with us, then you're investing in making an impact in these communities – not just Aboriginal communities but any community that touches Aboriginal communities." "That's the new narrative that we have to start sharing with Australia, it's about impact investment," said Carol. "If you work with Aboriginal business, we will always come from a place of country-centredness. Issues of climate change and sustainability will always be there front and centre because that's our country." At the centre of Carol's business, there is a connection to Country and community which echoes the sentiments of other Indigenous businesses that consider themselves inseparable from these values (Mrabure, 2019). Carol concludes, "government and corporates need to commit to implementing all aspects of the IPP at every level. They need to trust that Indigenous businesses can do this. If you look at the Indigenous business sector, it is headed up by people with incredible qualifications and experience. We don't just do cultural awareness training. It's amazing what is out there. I truly believe that if they applied all the Indigenous procurement policies, then the disadvantage gap would be absolutely reduced. There would be an acceleration of closing the gap." Carol firmly believes that Indigenous procurement policies can reduce the disadvantage gap, but government and organisations lack faith in Indigenous businesses and commitment to implementing these policies. This lack of faith in Indigenous people's capabilities represents the government's ongoing paternalistic approach towards policies that affect Indigenous Australians (Moreton-Robinson, 2015). To young Indigenous women aspiring to become an entrepreneur, Carol says – "If you want to be a social entrepreneur or businesswoman, back yourself and step into the space. When you do, let people know that you're there because there's a whole tribe of us ready to support you." Carol alludes to the importance of confidence in asserting one's place as an Indigenous businesswoman, as self-confidence is positively associated with entrepreneurial outcomes (Maczulskij & Viinikainen, 2023). Conclusions and Policy implications Carol's story is indicative of the unique value that Indigenous businesses can offer, and hence, the government should build their faith in Indigenous businesses and commit to Indigenous procurement policies. Furthermore, policies and initiatives that aim to reduce disadvantages should avoid imposing Western business models on definitions of Indigenous success (Mrabure, 2019). One way to avoid this would be to consult a business such as Carol's so that Indigenous voices are at the forefront of Indigenous concerns. Organisations should also ensure that Indigenous expertise is being valued and positioned at the appropriate level. Failure to do so results in ineffective initiatives and less participation of Indigenous people in business (Lahn, 2018). Due to gender-related barriers, programs specifically aimed at increasing the participation of women in business are crucial. These programs can foster skills and attributes such as resilience and self-confidence to withstand the obstacles and hardships in the process of entrepreneurship (Nate et al., 2022).

Social Entrepreneurship

Beyond its commercial ventures, Murawin also runs the "Morning Sky" project, which aims to give back to the community. The project focuses on financial and economic empowerment, with a particular emphasis on working with Indigenous women. "We conduct workshops about the power of business and how it can transform their lives," says Carol.

Murawin collaborates with both Commonwealth and State governments to integrate women into business conversations, helping them realize that they can engage in business at any level, tailored to their lifestyle and needs. Carol envisions empowering Indigenous women to become successful entrepreneurs and to build their self-confidence (Nate et al., 2022). She also challenges traditional views on work-life balance, asserting that entrepreneurship should align with personal values and lifestyles (Gherardi, 2015).

"We provide financial and in-kind support to organizations dedicated to empowering Indigenous girls and women," Carol shares. "For example, we are currently working with corporates to set up a scholarship for an Indigenous girl to attend boarding school. I always wanted that opportunity for consistent education, but it was something I never had."

Carol's commitment to educational empowerment is deeply personal, informed by her own experience of being denied opportunities for consistent education. Educational initiatives that support Indigenous youth are integral in improving life outcomes, particularly when approached from a relational, Indigenous perspective (Keddie, 2013).

Murawin's social impact extends to its pioneering efforts in addressing critical issues in the community. Carol recalls organizing a national conference to tackle the impacts of child sexual abuse, a cause she championed during her years working in child protection. "We funded a three-day national conference in Brisbane, aiming to bring awareness and create solutions for supporting communities affected by child sexual abuse," she says.

This initiative underscored the need for Indigenous leadership in addressing complex social issues. "It's about the thought leadership required to support the continued growth and thriving of Indigenous businesses," Carol notes, highlighting the gap in research that explores Indigenous business models in a contemporary context.

Addressing Challenges

"I'm very conscious of Murawin's identity as an Indigenous-led company," Carol says. "While we are an Indigenous-owned business, we strive to work in an intercultural space, employing both Indigenous and non-Indigenous people at all levels. We need both grassroots communicators and boardroom professionals."

As Murawin continues to grow, Carol faces the common challenges of cash flow and staffing. "Cash flow is always an issue. Large corporates take up to 90 days to pay, and while that's normal for them, it's a burden for a small company like ours," she says.

Hiring and retaining staff, especially qualified mid-to-senior-level Aboriginal professionals, is another challenge. "They're often running their own businesses or holding positions in government or corporates. Why would they come to a small Indigenous business?" Carol asks. To address this, she encourages professionals to take secondments, fostering knowledge exchange and capacity-building for both organizations.

Another significant hurdle for Indigenous businesses is access to finance. "We haven't approached banks for loans, preferring to use our own funds," Carol explains. "We've received a grant from Indigenous Business Australia (IBA), which we used during the COVID-19 crisis. We've made a deliberate choice to do this ourselves, as a statement of our independence."

Carol stresses that Indigenous businesses cannot afford to fail, both for their own survival and for the reputation of the broader Indigenous business community. "We can't afford to make mistakes. If we do, I feel as though other Indigenous businesswomen will be unfairly judged for it," she reflects. "To succeed, we have to provide 160% of the service to overcome biases related to race and gender."

Carol's commitment to excellence stems from a desire to counter implicit biases, as studies show that the work of minority groups is often undervalued (De Sante, 2013).

Recommendations for Change

Carol advocates for early intervention in teaching children about business and entrepreneurship. "My grandchildren, as young as five and six years old, have already started learning about business. They made $80 from collecting seeds for another Indigenous business, and their mother set up an account for them," she shares with pride. "At Murawin, I pay my children above the minimum wage for their small tasks because it's about breaking cycles of poverty."

Murawin has grown into a multi-million-dollar company, a success Carol attributes to her deep knowledge of public administration, research, and community engagement. "I had to reinvent myself, learn the language of business, and immerse myself in the sector. It wasn't easy," she admits. "But I had to stand up and shine, especially as an Aboriginal woman. It's hard to promote yourself when you're expected to be humble, but I had to do it."

Carol's journey resonates with the challenges faced by Indigenous women entrepreneurs, who encounter additional barriers to recognition and success (Lahn, 2018). Her story reflects the need for greater confidence, both in herself and in the broader Indigenous business community.

Changing Paradigms and Perceptions

Carol emphasizes the importance of seeing money and resources as tools for impact. "If you have access to resources, it's about creating change. When clients work with us, they're investing in making a meaningful impact, not just for Aboriginal communities but for all communities that are connected to Aboriginal peoples," she explains.

"We must shift the narrative," Carol argues. "If you invest in Indigenous businesses, you're also investing in sustainability, climate change solutions, and country-centred values."

Carol believes that Indigenous businesses have unique strengths, and that government and corporations must embrace these strengths. "The Indigenous business sector is led by people with incredible qualifications and experience. We don't just do cultural awareness training. There's so much more," she says. "If Indigenous procurement policies are implemented effectively, we could significantly reduce the disadvantage gap and accelerate change."

Carol firmly believes that implementing Indigenous procurement policies can address the disadvantage gap, but government and organizations must trust Indigenous businesses to lead. The ongoing paternalistic approach to Indigenous policies must be reconsidered (Moreton-Robinson, 2015).

Conclusion and Policy Implications

Carol's story highlights the valuable contributions Indigenous businesses can make and the need for greater government support. Policies should focus on empowering Indigenous businesses without imposing Western business models on Indigenous success (Mrabure, 2019). Consulting with Indigenous-led businesses like Murawin will ensure that Indigenous perspectives are at the forefront of decision-making.

Furthermore, gender-specific programs aimed at supporting Indigenous women in business are essential. These initiatives can help foster resilience and self-confidence, equipping women to overcome the challenges of entrepreneurship (Nate et al., 2022).

By recognizing Indigenous expertise, promoting economic empowerment, and supporting the growth of Indigenous women in business, we can drive systemic change that will benefit not only Indigenous communities but also Australian society as a whole.

References

ABS. (2021). *2021 Census – Employment, Income and Education*- external site opens in new window [TableBuilder], accessed 20 June 2022.

Baxter, L. P., & Meyers, N. M. (2016). Increasing urban Indigenous students' attendance: Mitigating the influence of poverty through community partnership. *Australian Journal of Education*, *60*(3), 211–228. https://doi.org/10.1177/0004944116664438

De Sante, C. D. (2013). Working twice as hard to get half as far: Race, Work Ethic, and America's Deserving Poor. *American Journal of Political Science*, *57*(2), 342–356. https://doi.org/https://doi.org/10.1111/ajps.12006

Dinku, Y., & Hunt, J. (2019). *Factors Associated with the Labour Force Participation of Prime-age Indigenous Australians*- external site opens in new window, Centre for Aboriginal Economic Policy Research, Australian National University, accessed 6 June 2023.

Fairlie, R. W., & Fossen, F. M. (2020). Defining Opportunity versus Necessity Entrepreneurship: Two Components of Business Creation. In S. W. Polachek & K. Tatsiramos (Eds.), *Change at Home, in the Labor Market, and On the Job* (Vol. 48, pp. 253–289). Emerald Publishing Limited. https://doi.org/10.1108/S0147-912120200000048008

Gherardi, S. (2015). Authoring the female entrepreneur while talking the discourse of work–family life balance. *International Small Business Journal*, *33*, 649–666. https://doi.org/10.1177/0266242614549780

Gobble, M. M. (2017). Innovation at the bottom of the pyramid. *Research-Technology Management*, *60*(3), 62–67. https://doi.org/10.1080/08956308.2017.1301006

Keddie, A. (2013). Schooling for self-determination through a justice politics of Indigenous representation. *International Journal of Qualitative Studies in Education*, *26*(1), 21–38. https://doi.org/10.1080/09518398.2011.604651

Lahn, J. (2018). Being indigenous in the bureaucracy: Narratives of work and exit. *International Indigenous Policy Journal*, *9*(1). https://doi.org/10.18584/iipj.2018.9.1.3

Maczulskij, T., & Viinikainen, J. (2023). Self-confidence predicts entrepreneurship and entrepreneurial success. *Journal of Business Venturing Insights*, *19*, e00382. https://doi.org/10.1016/j.jbvi.2023.e00382

Moreton-Robinson, A.(2015) The White Possessive: Property, Power, and Indigenous Sovereignty. *Indigenous Americas*, 272. University of Minnesota Press. www.jstor.org/stable/10.5749/j.ctt155jmpf

Mrabure, R. O. (2019). Indigenous business success: A hybrid perspective. *Journal of Enterprising Communities: People and Places in the Global Economy*, *13*(1/2), 24–41. https://doi.org/10.1108/JEC-10-2018-0076

Nate, S., Grecu, V., Stavytskyy, A., & Kharlamova, G. (2022). Fostering Entrepreneurial Ecosystems through the Stimulation and Mentorship of New Entrepreneurs. *Sustainability*, *14*, 7985. https://doi.org/10.3390/su14137985

Peredo, A. M., & McLean, M. (2010). Indigenous development and the cultural captivity of entrepreneurship. *Business & Society*, *52*(4), 592–620. https://doi.org/10.1177/0007650309356201

Shelton, L. M., & Lugo, M. V. (2021). The resilience of the minority and female entrepreneurs: A look at ethnicity and gender. *Journal of Developmental Entrepreneurship*, *26*(4). https://doi.org/10.1142/S1084946721500266

Silva-Laya, M., D'Angelo, N., García, E., Zúñiga, L., & Fernández, T. (2020). Urban poverty and education. A systematic literature review. *Educational Research Review*, *29*, 100280. https://doi.org/10.1016/j.edurev.2019.05.002

Thunig, A., & Jones, T. (2021). 'Don't make me play house-n***er': Indigenous academic women treated as 'black performer' within higher education. *The Australian Educational Researcher*, *48*(3), 397–417. https://doi.org/10.1007/s13384-020-00405-9

9 Rachelle Towart: Increasing the number of First Nations leaders in Executive Positions in Australia

www.pipelinetalent.com.au/

Meena Chavan, Jane Menzies, and Leanne Holt

Born in Blacktown NSW, Rachelle Towart was raised in Western Sydney before moving to Canberra. As a proud Wonnarua woman from Singleton NSW, Rachelle is passionate about empowering Aboriginal and/or Torres Strait Islander people to take up leadership positions.

Rachelle founded Pipeline Talent which specialises in executive level recruitment for First Nations leaders. Pipeline Talent is 100% Indigenous owned and connects exceptional First Nations professionals with executive level opportunities in corporate, community, academia and government sectors across Australia. After launching the business in 2016, Rachelle received an OAM (Order of Australia Medal) for her service to the Aboriginal community (2018)

Before Rachelle founded Pipeline Talent, she held the CEO position at the Aboriginal Indigenous Leadership Centre where she received numerous awards including the Westpac Community CEO of the Year (2014).

Motivations for business

Rachelle wanted a better life than what her parents could give her. "My parents had almost nothing," said Rachelle. "I wanted to do things that they weren't able to do, like buy my own home and have money that I could buy things with."

"We'd always lived in government housing. My mum still lives in government housing. I really wanted to have my own home," Rachelle explained. "I knew that I was going to have to work really hard to be able to do that."

Early Life

Rachelle disliked school as a child. "I was a bit of a ratbag as a kid," she said. Just getting by, she completed year 10. Rachelle wanted to be a hairdresser while she was at school. Her aunt told her that if she wanted to be a hairdresser, she needed to volunteer at a local hairdressing salon. "Well, I lasted

DOI: 10.4324/9781003386230-9

until lunchtime of day one. Sweeping up people's hair on the floor wasn't what I had pictured."

She was given two choices – she could go back to school, or she could go get a job. She enrolled in TAFE and studied a secretarial studies course. There she quickly learnt how to use a typewriter and shorthand. Before finishing her qualification, she was offered multiple jobs. "I was being offered jobs more than my mum and dad's incomes combined," said Rachelle.

She worked as a secretary for several years. Her first Aboriginal employer, Dawn, encouraged her to go back to school. "Rachelle, if you want to get further in the world, you need to go back to school," said Dawn.

"Because of her, I went and did year 11 and 12 at night," said Rachelle. From there, Rachelle went on to do a few different learning and developing programs paid for by her work. Slowly, she began to climb up the ranks of public service jobs. "I always thought that I wanted to become a public servant because they got a car park spot that was reserved for senior roles," said Rachelle.

In 2004, she was rejected for a promotion that she had applied for. A friend of hers encouraged her to move on and apply for a job at the Australian Indigenous Leadership Centre instead. She got the job and was appointed as a Business Manager. With 12 months of leave without pay, Rachelle left the public service and moved into the not-for-profit world. "About three months in, I realised that I'd made the best career decision in my life," she said.

A few years later, Rachelle was offered the role of CEO. "There was $14,000 in funds for the AILC to distribute and not much else," she said. Despite this, she stayed because she knew that the Australian Indigenous Leadership Centre had the power to change the lives of Aboriginal and Torres Strait Islander people. Rachelle mentioned, "We knew that 25 started, 25 finished, and 15 received their first-ever educational qualification. Ten may not have been able to read or write, but we knew that 70% of them went on to further education. 70% also received their first $15,000-16,000 pay increase within the first 12 months of completing the program."

It was something that Rachelle knew was worth saving. She wrote to Auntie Gail, the CEO of Westpac at the time, "Dear Auntie Gail, I'd like to have lunch with you and ten of your rich friends." From there, Rachelle managed to recover and build the organisation into something she could be proud of. Being the CEO of an educational non-for-profit came with its ups and downs, but no day was ever the same.

By 2016, she was ready for her next career move. She was encouraged to apply for a Senior Executive Service (SES) position at the Department of the Prime Minister and Cabinet (PM&C). "I went, okay, that would get me a car park spot," said Rachelle. Within 48 hours after applying, she was offered a position. She was unsure about whether she wanted the role.

At the time, Rachelle was doing great things in the world of leadership development. As part of her role as a board member, Rachelle flew to Western

Australia. During the flight, she read an article about herself in the Qantas in-flight magazine. She sat there and asked herself, "Am I going to take this government job to get a car park?"

She turned the page and read an article about women in the pipeline. There was still a long way to go concerning the number of women employed in corporate, community, and government sectors. "I thought, if I replaced the word 'woman' with 'Aboriginal and Torres Strait Islander people', where would the numbers sit?"

"It flatlined by the time I did a quick calculation in my head of the number of Aboriginal and Torres Strait Islander people competing for C-Suite jobs across the country, in ASX listed companies, in board positions, in universities, in state and federal government, in more than 50% of Aboriginal organisations being run by non-Aboriginal people." She thought, "I've created this group of Aboriginal leaders across the country. I know that we have access to them. Why aren't they getting the opportunities in leadership roles?"

By the time she had gotten off the plane, she made her decision. She called the minister and said, "Minister, I'm not taking the job. I'm going to start a recruitment company." Rather than becoming the 23rd Aboriginal public servant at that time, she decided to create 23 roles instead.

The Early Days of Pipeline Talent

When she started the company, Rachelle knew nothing about recruitment. She thought, "how hard could it be?" She realised quickly that the industry was just like the used car sales and real estate industry. It was all driven by money. She spoke to people in the industry and asked how to become a recruiter. She learnt that apart from a few "cert twos" and "cert fours", there weren't any educational qualifications for recruitment.

"Nothing I had done previously would be recognised." Despite being awarded an Order of Australia Medal, and many other awards and accolades, none of her accomplishments were recognised in the recruitment industry.

"Four months into the business, I didn't do anything relating to recruitment." Instead, Rachelle worked with the Minister to review remote Indigenous housing and worked with Lifeline on Indigenous suicide prevention. "I was doing a whole heap of things that weren't related to recruitment because that was the easy thing to do, I knew how to do that."

Soon after, Rachelle got a phone call from her mum – "Come and get your brother's baby."

"What baby?" asked Rachelle.

At that time, Rachelle's daughter was 22, and Rachelle and her husband had been married for 24 years. She wasn't expecting to have to take care of another baby.

Shortly after, she found herself with a four-month-old baby. "My brother, unfortunately, is a drug addict and has been for a number of years," said Rachelle. "The baby was supposed to be with me for two weeks."

A few months later, baby number two arrived. With two babies born in the same year, Rachelle was unsure about what she should do – call the Minister and ask for a job, or continue pursuing her recruitment business?

She chose the hard way. Rachelle knew that she needed to get in and give it a fair crack. She knew that it was needed in the world. It was needed in her community.

The recruitment agencies wouldn't teach Rachelle how to do it, so she went undercover. She went to a recruitment agency and asked for a job. "I realised that there were many agencies out there that just thought about the money that they were going to make for me and my placement. They were going to use me and my Aboriginality in the placement, and they were going to get a shit ton of money from it." By going undercover, Rachelle learnt what not to do.

For Rachelle, recruitment is about more than just project management and building relationships. It's about "telling a story about the passion that [she] has behind getting people into executive roles".

"I still haven't cracked it," said Rachelle. "I want to see that I placed my first ever Aboriginal candidate in an ASX listed role in a C-Suite position."

"There's only one woman at the top at the moment in the top 200," she said. "We've got 0.04% of Aboriginal and Torres Strait Islander people in executive roles in our country, and that needs to change."

"That's why Pipeline Talent is around. We're still the only employment agency that leads recruitment processes for roles upwards of$100,000 in salary. That's where we sit in our realm," continues Rachelle. "People ask me all the time to do labour-hire and other stuff. I just say, no. We're really good at what we do."

Challenges

As the eldest child of four, Rachelle feels a great sense of responsibility for her younger siblings. "My sisters and I are very entrepreneurial," she said. "My next sister lives in Townsville and her husband has a car dealership."

Rachelle's other sister left home for a three-month transfer and has never been back since. "Her girls are adults now and I'm putting them through university," said Rachelle.

"We have a great support network around us but nobody's volunteering to look after the kids. We know that's our responsibility. It will change when they get older but nobody wants to look after toddlers."

At the age of 14, her cousin was one of the youngest people to be contracted for the NSW rugby league back in the day. "But he didn't get out. He got dealt a harder life," she said. "He was a heroin addict by the time he was 19."

"Drugs were all around us as kids and my family has always been influenced by drugs. My brother was probably 16–17 when he first tried drugs. Now he's 45 and he hasn't got a home. He's got five children that he's never had responsibility for," said Rachelle. "But we still love him."

"[His] children have a lot of challenges ahead," she explains. "Because they're trauma babies and have been abused by drugs, there's a whole heap of stuff that they've got in front of them."

"Everybody says that it's really great that we've done that, but I wouldn't change it for the world," said Rachelle.

"It has made me a better business owner because I hire other women who have had challenges that other people might not look so favourably on when hiring," said Rachelle. "That's why my team is so important to me. The old saying, 'teamwork makes the dream work' is a really big thing for me."

"I've got ex-public servants that work for me. They almost volunteer for me because they love what we do. They all just love the idea that while we are a for-profit business, we still have the social responsibility piece."

Policy directions recommended by Rachelle

When asked how and what Indigenous communities are struggling to get top positions?

Rachelle's opinion was that " and until now, Indigenous communities have struggled to reach the top positions at the top multinational corporations and government organizations. Rachelle believes that this is because Australia isn't ready. They don't trust Indigenous people to take up these roles.

"We've just had our first Australian woman prime minister. Look how well that went," said Rachelle. "Will Australians want another female prime minister soon?" she asks. "I don't know that they're ready for that again anytime soon."

"In one of the minister's offices, there was a painting in one of the meeting rooms depicting what an Aboriginal prime minister would look like," said Rachelle. "Unfortunately, it was male. A young, handsome, Aboriginal guy."

"Is Australia ready for an Aboriginal prime minister?" asked Rachelle. "Hell no."

"Are they ready to trust Aboriginal people in leadership roles? I have a question mark over that all the time," she said. "We see more than 50% of Aboriginal businesses being run by non-Aboriginal people. Why?"

Pipeline Talent

"That's my passion and drive, to make that change," said Rachelle. "This is why I think we've been so successful. We're looking for diamonds in the rough."

"We're not a dump and run recruitment agency," she explains. "Some people come in and pay 18% of somebody's first year of wages as remuneration for placing a person. Then they just dump them and run."

"One of the big things that we do differently is that we provide our candidates with their first 100 days of coaching as part of the replacement," said Rachelle. "We don't charge any additional money for it."

Rachel often gets contacted by recruitment agencies asking for Aboriginal candidates. "No, I'm not giving them to you. You don't deserve them. You don't look after them," says Rachelle.

"One of my biggest challenges against the big executive recruiters is that everybody knows that I'm an Aboriginal business."

As an Aboriginal business, Rachelle believes that others don't trust her as much as her competitors. "Trust is a really big thing for Aboriginal businesses," she says. "For the Indigenous Procurement Policy (IPP) to work, people need to trust Aboriginal businesses."

"If I were just an Aboriginal recruiter that did labour-hire, entry-level recruitment, I would probably get 1,000 times more work than what we do now."

The IPP, explains Rachelle, only deals with entry-level roles. "How are we recruiting at all levels? How are we using service providers at all levels?" asks Rachelle.

Recommendations from Rachelle

"My policy recommendation would be that the IPP needs to include all levels, not just entry-level," said Rachelle. "It's like we're only recruiting Aboriginal people in entry levels."

"We don't want to be the token change either," said Rachelle "I know that my candidates, the people that we have daily dealings with, want to be known because they can do the job. Their culture is just a bonus." She elaborates, "they don't want to be appointed because they're Aboriginal into an executive role. They want to be appointed into an executive role because they can do the job."

"Aboriginal people are some of the most trained people in the world," she said. "If you ask people for their list of qualifications, compared to their counterparts, they will have 20 against two."

"But we still have to do more training."

"I don't like mentoring programs, they're not for me. I'm more about coaching a specific skill set," she said. "If you've got a skill gap, how do you correct that?"

"We need specific coaching programs that do an individual assessment and identify their skill gaps," said Rachelle.

"For me, you need to look at the end goal," she said. "If young people are thinking about starting a business, they need to think about what skill gaps they have to reach their goal."

Changing decision-makers attitudes

The prevailing stigmas about Indigenous people continue to inhibit success. Top-down reform is required to change the minds of key decision-makers and to get them to trust Aboriginal people.

"I sit on the Supply Nations Indigenous Business Advisory Group and have access to some amazing Aboriginal businesses," said Rachelle. "Some of them have moved away from selling themselves as an Aboriginal business because the label can bring them down their chances of accessing contracts and winning tenders."

As an Indigenous business, Rachelle's company is often asked to put in a tender application for Federal government recruitment jobs. Each time, from the same department, she receives the same response – "Thank you for your application. On this occasion, we're using the same people that we used last time."

"They require me to meet their quota saying that they've gone out to an Aboriginal business," she states.

"I have, more or less, said to the head of the department, please take me off your list of people," said Rachelle. "You can use the IPP to come to me directly if your recruitment team knew how the policy worked."

"No matter what I've done for this government department, they simply choose to ignore it," she said. "They use their own non-Indigenous recruitment team, and they get the same people, over and over again."

"How are things going to change when the government refuses to engage with businesses and Indigenous people beyond entry-level?" she asks. "If the government at that level doesn't trust an Aboriginal business to run their executive recruitment process for them, how are we going to change at NAB or Rio Tinto?"

"Yet they say, look how much we're spending on Aboriginal businesses!" said Rachelle. "I question where that money is being spent. It's at entry-level jobs, not executive roles."

Success

"I will know that I'm successful when I fly into Sydney, Melbourne, New York, London, look at one of these buildings in lights at night, and know that an Aboriginal person is leading that company," said Rachelle.

"I think that if you believe in something enough, and you're committed, and you can see it making a difference, then all your dreams will come true," she said. "Walt Disney famously said, 'If you don't have a dream, how can a dream come true?' "

"The dream that I had is coming true. It hasn't come true yet, but I know that I'm closer than I was six years ago," said Rachelle. "I'm not about to give up on it. I can't give up on it because they are coming."

Conclusions

Rachelle's observations of Indigenous under-representation at the executive level reflect a broader culture of exclusion and discrimination within the workforce, as highlighted by Hunter and Shirodkhar (2019). In a cross-sectional examination of the factors that underpin Indigenous economic participation, they highlight the role of the non-Indigenous "in-group" in granting access to key elements of social capital, such as "networks and successful mentors and role models." Further, a study of Indigenous employment at varying levels by Minderoo Foundation (2022) highlighted that only 0.7% of leadership positions (across 31 surveyed companies) were held by Indigenous employees.

Thus, Rachelle's emphasis on coaching and support throughout the first 100 days of placement is a critical factor in enhancing Indigenous participation beyond entry level roles.

While the introduction of policy based measures such as the IPP have enhanced Indigenous economic activity (Hudson, 2017), scholars (Hudson, 2017; Shirodkar & Hunter, 2019) provide support to Rachelle's experience, recognising that the policy framework may leave Indigenous businesses being treated as a quota, rather than as a meaningful partnership opportunity. Since the IPP came into effect in 2015–16, the government has spent around $2 billion on procurement contracts for Indigenous businesses (Shirodkar & Hunter, 2019).

Hudson (2017) highlights that the IPP is inherently "limited to only providing opportunities for Indigenous businesses that are aligned with the government's procurement requirements." They argue that in order to "future-proof" the Indigenous business sector, strategies need to exist beyond political cycles and government tenders. Hudson (2017) also notes that due to the lack of regulation or penalty on whether Indigenous quotas are met, many companies are treating Indigenous procurement as a "tick-box exercise." Similarly, data from the Minderoo Foundation, 2022 that showed only 76% of businesses had Indigenous employment targets, and only 67% of these provided any ongoing reporting about meeting and retaining such targets.

In order to foster the growth of Indigenous talent in leadership and executive positions, both Rachelle and scholars in the field acknowledge the importance of policy that supports upward mobility, rather than filling quotas and upholding the existing status quo. Through her business, Rachelle is actively supporting talented First Nations leaders to be employed in roles that allow them to fulfill their greatest potential.

References

Hudson, S. (2017). 'Future Proofing' the Indigenous business sector. *Policy: A Journal of Public Policy and Ideas*, *33*(2), 3–7.

Minderoo Foundation. (2022). *Australian Indigenous employment index*. Retrieved 12/03/2024 from www.minderoo.org/indigenous-employment-index/

Shirodkar, S., & Hunter, B. (2019). Factors underlying the likelihood of being in business for Indigenous and non-Indigenous Australians *Australian Journal of Labour Economics*, *22*(1), 5–27. https://doi.org/10.3316/ielapa.017682708350484

10 Amanda Healy: Empowering Indigenous Designers Through Fashion and Social Enterprise

https://kirrikin.com/

Meena Chavan, Jane Menzies, and Leanne Holt

Where luxury clothing accessories meet contemporary Indigenous Australian art.

Amanda Healy, a proud Koori woman from the Wonnarua nation of the Hunter Valley, New South Wales, currently resides in Perth, Western Australia. After gaining extensive experience in the mining and engineering industries, Amanda went on to establish two successful social enterprises—Kirrikin and Warrikal. Kirrikin collaborates with Indigenous artists to feature their artwork on handmade, sustainable clothing, with designs often representing Songlines, cultural stories, and the personal identities of the artists. The Koori people, originally from areas spanning both NSW and Victoria, have a rich and enduring culture that is expressed through Songlines, art, and oral traditions (Ryan, 2015).

Early Years

From a young age, Amanda's father instilled in her a deep sense of resilience and self-sufficiency. "He was a solid worker with a great work ethic. I think he instilled that in all of us," Amanda shared. "He is always my inspiration. I admire what he did at a time when it was incredibly difficult to be an Aboriginal Australian. It was nearly impossible to be effectively trained in a profession and hold down a job for many years while battling his own struggles around identity and the broader narrative about Aboriginal people."

Amanda's father's influence reflects the strength found in family ties, a theme seen in Hickey's (2021) research, where participants noted that family support helps them overcome adversity. Connection to family, community, and mentors has been shown to enhance well-being (Hickey, 2021).

Her father also had a profound cultural connection to the land. "Although it wasn't his country, he always respected the local Aboriginal communities. He loved fishing and taught us how to find food in the bush, how to stay safe, and recognize potential dangers," Amanda recalled.

DOI: 10.4324/9781003386230-10

Studies have found that a connection to country and culture contributes positively to the well-being of Indigenous people, acting as a protective factor (Hickey, 2021; Sangha et al., 2015).

Working Years

At the age of 14, like many Aboriginal people of her generation, Amanda left school to work. Over the years, she took on various jobs, including pulling prawn heads, working in a corner shop, and sales positions. At 21, she secured her first stable office job with the Commonwealth Employment Service in Geraldton Western Australia.

Her career trajectory continued with a role as a recruiting officer at BHP, where she worked for over a decade. "My dad had worked in the mining industry for most of his life, and he encouraged me to gain these skills and experiences. We often talked about the industry, and it became something we shared and laughed about together," Amanda said.

During her time at BHP, Amanda helped develop BHP operations in Australia, Indonesia, Africa, and Canada, where she worked on the development of Canadian diamond mines. While in Canada, she fell pregnant, but the relationship didn't work out, and she returned to Australia to have her son, as a single mother.

Amanda was frustrated by the lack of autonomy in her role. "I always felt like a square peg in a round hole," she said. "I didn't like being told what to do or how to do it."

"I felt limited at BHP, especially as an Aboriginal woman. They didn't know what to do with me. I would check the box 'Do you identify as Aboriginal?' every year, but that was the extent of their engagement with my identity."

This experience highlights the challenges of multi-dimensional discrimination that Indigenous women face, where gender and race intersect to create systems of inequity. Amanda's experience aligns with Leon's (2022) findings that Indigenous women often encounter barriers in career advancement due to unconscious biases.

"People would look at me and say, 'You don't look Aboriginal, you're too pretty.' I'm not sure they would have known what to do with me even if I didn't meet their expectations," Amanda said. When declaring my Aboriginality to people, I was very often told in a scoffing tone "You are not Aboriginal" – which caused me to eventually stop telling people I was Aboriginal – which is now interesting, because they 'why didn't you tell me' – it is quite funny!

After returning to Australia, Amanda spent some time in Perth working for various companies. However, she grew frustrated with long hours and a lack of time with her son. "As a single mum, I worked from 7am to 7pm just to pay the bills, leaving little time for my son," she shared.

In 2004, a friend approached her to help start a new business. "I thought it would give me more freedom and time, but after a few years my then business partner left, and I took over the business," Amanda explained.

Building a Business

In 2009, Amanda registered her business under Supply Nation, a government initiative that connects Indigenous businesses to the supply chains of government and large organizations (Supply Nation, 2023; Collins & Norman, 2018). This initiative aims to promote Indigenous entrepreneurship and provide access to critical business resources.

In 2014, Amanda founded Kirrikin as a social enterprise after being frustrated with the lack of authentic Indigenous fashion options available. "I searched for a scarf to represent my heritage, but everything I found was inauthentic—mass-produced overseas with no connection to the culture," Amanda said.

Determined to change this, Amanda began printing authentic Aboriginal art on luxury fabrics, aiming to create high-quality, culturally respectful pieces. "It became clear that I couldn't ethically profit from the artists unless I made sure they were fairly compensated for their work," she explained.

Kirrikin's model supports Indigenous communities by providing opportunities for economic empowerment. "I support single mothers and anyone in need, offering financial assistance where I can," Amanda said.

The name "Kirrikin," meaning "Sunday's best clothes" in Wonnarua, reflects Amanda's heritage and the pride she takes in her culture. She believes that through luxury fashion, she can challenge negative stereotypes about Indigenous people and showcase the richness of their culture.

Through Kirrikin, Amanda aims to change perceptions of Indigenous culture, ensuring that it is represented authentically. This resonates with Chow et al. (2022), who note that art intermediaries can protect cultural integrity while sharing cultural stories.

Kirrikin's focus on sustainability aligns with broader trends in slow fashion, as Amanda emphasizes creating garments that last a lifetime. "I only do one collection a year and ensure that each item is timeless, not part of the fast-fashion cycle," she said. Her sustainable approach mirrors the values of many Indigenous businesses, which integrate environmental knowledge into their practices (Chakraborty & Sadachar, 2023).

Kirrikin was named one of the top 10 designs to watch by *Elle* magazine in 2022, and the brand has gained recognition both in Australia and internationally, participating in fashion weeks in cities such as Sydney, London, Auckland, and Brussels.

Success and Education

Despite not receiving formal education until later in life, Amanda has achieved significant professional success. In 2016, she pursued an MBA at Curtin

University, not out of necessity, but to prove to herself that she could succeed academically. "I wanted to prove that I have the intellectual capacity to work through complex problems," she said.

After completing her MBA, Amanda was named an Adjunct Professor at Curtin University and awarded an Honorary Doctor of Commerce in 2020. In 2022, she was inducted into the WA Women's Hall of Fame for her contributions to her community, history, and culture.

Alongside her fashion endeavors, Amanda co-founded Warrikal, a commercial enterprise with a social conscience and a strong commitment to providing employment opportunities for Indigenous Australians. Today, Warrikal has nearly 1000 employees, 10% of whom are Aboriginal. The company also prioritizes hiring ex-inmates, supporting their reintegration into society after serving their sentences.

Challenges and Overcoming Barriers

For many Indigenous women entrepreneurs, success can be perceived as a threat by their communities. "Some women face harsh judgment, but I've been fortunate not to experience this as intensely," Amanda said. "I always try to support other Aboriginal women in business and work collaboratively with them."

Access to financial support remains a significant challenge. Amanda notes that traditional financial institutions often don't understand the unique needs of small Indigenous businesses. "Banks make it nearly impossible to get the funding you need to run a successful business," she explained.

Recommendations for Government and Industry Support

Amanda advocates for increased access to non-traditional, low-risk funding for Indigenous entrepreneurs. "We've been advocating for 15 years for funding that doesn't require sharing unreasonable amounts of risk," she said. "The current system places all the risk on the individual."

She also emphasizes the need for culturally relevant education and training that supports Indigenous entrepreneurs at all stages of their careers. This includes addressing the structural barriers in education that limit access to Indigenous knowledge and perpetuate Western systems and values (Street et al., 2022).

Moreover, Amanda recommends policies to reduce employment inequality by restricting the use of criminal records in hiring decisions, especially where the conviction is not relevant to the role (Naylor & Heydon, 2022).

Conclusion

Amanda Healy's journey exemplifies the power of entrepreneurship to create positive change in communities. Despite the numerous challenges she has faced, her focus remains on her mission to support her people and reshape perceptions of Indigenous culture.

"Being an entrepreneur gives me the freedom to make a real impact on my community," she said. "It's not about me; it's about the teams that support my vision and the people I can help along the way."

References

Chakraborty, S., & Sadachar, A. (2023). Can a connection with the Indigenous cultural values encourage sustainable apparel consumption? *Journal of Fashion Marketing and Management*, *27*(1), 80–99. https://doi.org/10.1108/JFMM-07-2021-0191

Chow, A. M., Carrington, M., & Ozanne, J. L. (2022). Reimagining the Indigenous art market: Site of decolonisation and assertion of Indigenous cultures. *Journal of Marketing Management*, *38*(17–18), 1983–2010. https://doi.org/10.1080/0267257X.2022.2082513

Collins, J., & Norman, H. (2018). Indigenous entrepreneurship and Indigenous employment in Australia. *Journal of Australian Political Economy*, *82*, 149–170. www.ppesydney.net/content/uploads/2020/05/Indigenous-entrepreneurship-and-indigenous-employment-in-Australia.pdf

Hickey, S. (2021). Talking back to the research: Indigenous wellbeing and resilience narratives from Urban Australia. *Journal of Human Development and Capabilities*, *22*(3), 423–445. https://doi.org/10.1080/19452829.2021.1882966

Leon, C. (2022). Insights for Indigenous employment into a case study of unconscious bias in the Australian Public Service. *Australian Journal of Social Issues*, *57*(4), 898–919. https://doi.org/https://doi.org/10.1002/ajs4.221

Naylor, B., & Heydon, G. (2022). Criminal records, discrimination, and Aboriginal communities: Enhancing employment opportunities. *Journal of Criminology*, *55*(4), 514–531. https://doi.org/10.1177/26338076221128996

Ryan, R. (2015). Tracing the Urban Songlines: Contemporary Koori Music in Melbourne. *Perfect Beat*, *2*(1), 20–37. https://doi.org/10.1558/prbt.v2i1.28799

Sangha, K. K., Le Brocque, A., Costanza, R., & Cadet-James, Y. (2015). Ecosystems and indigenous well-being: An integrated framework. *Global Ecology and Conservation*, *4*, 197–206. https://doi.org/https://doi.org/10.1016/j.gecco.2015.06.008

Street, C., Guenther, J., Smith, J., Robertson, K., Ludwig, W., Motlap, S., Woodroffe, T., Ober, R., Gillan, K., & Larkin, S. (2022). Do numbers speak for themselves? Exploring the use of quantitative data to measure policy 'success' in historical Indigenous higher education in the Northern Territory, Australia. *Race Ethnicity and Education*, *25*(3), 309–330. https://doi.org/10.1080/13613324.2021.2019003

Supply Nation. (2023). *Why Supply Nation?* Retrieved 14/03/2024 from https://supplynation.org.au/benefits/government/?gclid=CjwKCAjw0ZiiBhBKEiwA4PT9z4MNyc9XYRZ708hk0Frh129YHQbeBvU1cL_iLYkqaIkfyWDqddjBcRoCX-cQAvD_BwE#perks

11 Fran Dobbie: A filmmaker of Aboriginal Issues

https://earthstarproductions.com.au/home/

Meena Chavan, Jane Menzies, and Leanne Holt

Fran Dobbie, Director of Earthstar Productions, is a renowned film producer who brings inner strength and awareness through the medium of interactive workshops and television. As a producer, she is conscious of projects that connect, liaise, and consult with the Aboriginal community. Fran has a background in education and charity organisations, which led her to where she is today. Earthstar Productions has produced a range of films, television shows and advertisements centring on Aboriginal Identity and Aboriginal issues.

Early Life

Fran Dobbie is an Aboriginal woman from Yuin country on the South Coast of New South Wales. The totem of the Yuin people is the 'black swan', and many of her mother's relatives are still living there on Country. Fran was born in Western Sydney; her mother was from the Stolen Generation but she kept quiet about it as she did not want her three children to know about it. *"My mother was part of the Stolen Generation and she spent many times running away and hiding."*

As a child, Fran went through many challenges because of her mother and father's illnesses. *"There was always the ambulance coming from the hospital."* Apart from those issues, she cherished her childhood and recalls some fond memories of spending time with her Aboriginal family. *"They'd visit us and sit there and we had these yarns, my uncle would be playing the harmonica and there'd be someone with a baby breastfeeding and they were talking and laughing. It was really lovely way of being, something that I don't see now in families if I go into a community."* She was brought up as a Catholic and the religiosity in the community was dominant at that time.

Fran's great-great uncle was "Burnum Burnum", who is a historical figure and was quite well known for his bravery. Similarly, in 1926 her great-great grandmother, Jane Duran, had also contributed to the community by writing a letter to King George V, when children and her grandchildren were excluded and taken out of the local primary school. She later started five to six schools

DOI: 10.4324/9781003386230-11

which helped in the educational development of that local society on the South Coast of NSW. It influenced Fran as well as she went into the field of teaching and education. Both Burnum Burnum and Jane Duran were known as 'Political Warriors'.

Early Career

In the early stages of her career, Fran performed two jobs: one in the PR and Accounts department in a hospital, and the other one related to importing and exporting. *"Wherever I would apply for work, interestingly, I didn't even have any qualifications and I always got the job."* She was a self-motivated individual right from the start and knew the art of getting the job done. "*I observe, I take my time, but I do learn, and so I was very fortunate on my journey."*

After that, she decided that she wanted to become a teacher. *"I wanted to become a teacher because I'm a bit of a bossy boots and I like to educate."* She also knew that she had excellent communication skills and she could contribute more as an educator. She graduated with a distinction and acquired three degrees. *"I was proud of myself, obviously, because I couldn't believe that I even could do that but I did and with two children, I was a single mother at that stage, so it was really hard."* She was also working part-time while studying at the university, because she also had to manage her financial situation: *"I had a double mortgage because it was a breakup situation, I was very determined and there was something inside my spirit that just kept me going and going."*

After her graduation, she became a teacher and was selected for a workshop in New Mexico as part of the World Indigenous People's Conference. She considered herself to be a different sort of teacher than others. *"I was always a very different type of teacher and I like to include self-esteem and resilience-building skills within my teaching models, which sets me apart from others."*

She had a unique style of teaching in which she integrated nature into her classrooms. *"I always took the children out to experience Mother Nature, Mother Earth and then I would integrate that into what they were learning, whether it was Maths, Science, or English. Kids love being in my class, I mean that, we used to have a lot of fun."*

She decided to write a book as she wanted to share her writings with others. "I wrote this book called "Whisper". The book consisted of short stories about the journeys of two girls, a non-Aboriginal and the other Aboriginal. *"The Aboriginal girl was a combination of myself and my mother."* The stories included a lot of personal reflections from her childhood and conversations with her mother. *"But she (Fran's mother) never read my book. I think sometimes some of the truth came out, and so it was too much for her."* I was told after my mother passed away by my uncle that my mother didn't want me to make a 'loud noise and be heard' as someone may come and take me away, so she dumbed down any success I had.

Fran later published another book, "Paper Bags and Dreams."

Start of Fran's Entrepreneurial Journey

Fran then moved from being a full-time teacher to a part-time teacher and started a charity. As a teacher, she was aware of the bullying that was going around in the classrooms, and she decided to do something about it. "*The children were always fighting and arguing in the playground and classroom. I remember being really upset about all that (bullying), and I implemented self-esteem skills in my classroom which lead me to start a charity. I thought that I'm going to start a charity that focused on resilience and self-esteem because my teaching style on that subject worked very well in my classroom.*"

Initially, she knew that she did not have the skills required to manage and run the charity but she developed a network that helped her in understanding the dynamics. "*I kept meeting the right people, I always believed that the powers that be will just keep drawing me to these people.*"

It was initially quite hard to scale the idea and she had to face some rejections as well. "*I remember that when I put in the application form to the government to get my DGR (Deductible Gift Recipient) status, it was rejected, so we failed, and I remember crying. I was so upset that I thought I worked so hard.*" Later she managed to get in contact with someone in the government who helped in overcoming these obstacles to help Fran gain her DGR status. It was a big achievement as this status type had never been given before to a charity and the status helped in getting things on track and the charity grew.

She was always innovative and creative with her ideas, such as the following business idea:

> "*I remember this one day, I went to one of the big corporates and I was presenting the program of the self-esteem and resilience building model I used in my charity to the Executive staff. I explained to them that every child will receive little cue cards, on how you deal with anger, anti-bullying skills and calming techniques. The cue cards explored anger for example and included things such as where does it sit in your body, what does it look like, what does it sound like, what does it feel like, so then they were to do activities and gained self-reflective personal tools to sustain them through life. They would actually do the activities when they could feel the anger and then bring it up to be aware of it, where in their body, for example, the cue card was an anchoring tool, so they could take it home and put it on their wall or have it in their wallet as a constant reminder of skills to practise, a visual tool that was feeding their sub-conscious all the time, there was interactive music and dance, so it was all fun. The workshops were very entertaining while learning.*"

The idea was picked up by a big corporation who funded the charity and Fran became the face of it. The charity helped her in travelling all over Australia and soon its scope started to expand.

The Board of the charity comprised only one female (herself) as CEO and Board members, it had a steering committee consisting of other teachers.

Some big names in the industry were part of the Advisory committee and provided great support and advice which pushed her towards success. *"On the advisory committee, we had people like Jeff McMullen (Australian journalist, author and TV presenter) who would advise me privately, so it was quite outstanding for someone like me who never had any skills to do that having his expertise and guidance."*

During the recession years, the funding was diminished, so it became extremely difficult to survive in those circumstances: *"It was so hard, I'll never forget it, that day I lost my charity (job), my home and my car all in a 24-hour period, it was very sad to walk away from the charity I loved and worked so hard to establish had been taken over by another entity."* However, the experience and learning she gained from it were valuable which stayed with her forever.

It turned out to be a turning point in her life as she started to work on TV where she conducted these workshops with children. *"It was very successful, then they offered me a 13-part TV series. I did the 13-part TV series, and we took young people from high school on many experiences and adventures, while working with everyday challenging issues such as dealing with anger, bullying, issues of isolation and how to set boundaries."* It was shown on ABC and other top channels.

She decided to do TV documentaries, comedies, and short films. *"I just finished my first feature film titled 'Mother Mountain' in 2022 and it was presented in the Independent cinemas across Australia. I'm about to embark on another big feature film which will be an International film."* All her projects have linked some sort of social issues such as domestic violence and drug abuse. *"I always want to present important social issues into my films, that when people watch them they get a feeling of 'I can make a difference and a change'.*

She now has two companies, one is related to film production and the other is related to motivational and self-esteem /leadership workshops that she conducts.

She has transitioned from running a charity to running a business. *'I was the CEO of the charity, now I've got a proprietary limited company, sometimes I find it very, very difficult to get funding. I do other jobs to support myself personally while I continue to follow my passion of storytelling and producing films."* Although there is a difference in getting and managing finances, Fran has adapted swiftly. *"Getting the money from the government, I find very hard, I can go and get loans, if I have to, but then I have to make sure I have enough work that can maintain paying the bills back without being a charity."*

Fran found her passion for filmmaking and wants to spend most of her time and energy in storytelling. *"To be able to get keep my passion alive, filmmaking is a pathway to tell powerful stories that make a difference to audiences here in Australia and world-wide. I know that sitting down and having a good yarn can be a place of learning and growth, especially the challenges our world faces at this moment. Strange times. For me positive stories are the only thing that have power and strength that can be listened to by the people and felt by the people. Then the people can take some kind of action themselves via the internal messages felt through storytelling thus making decisions that will empower themselves and the world at large."*

Challenges

For Fran, the biggest challenge is related to the finances of the projects. *"I suppose the challenge for me is definitely the money."* Many of the big businesses that have come forward to offer support charge high fees. Therefore, she believes that the government needs to introduce some sort of package for small businesses such as Fran's.

When she lost her house, car, and job in a matter of a day. She remembers *"I remember sitting at a café, my friend had to come and pick me up and she drove me home and I had no house, so I had to live in my friend's house. My son had to sleep on the floor."*

She had to put money into the business from her own pocket which had an adverse impact on her financial health. *"I have put so much of my own money into my business. My business owes me a lot of money and I mean hundreds of thousands of dollars."* She only took a wage in her Charity work job; therefore, she had suffered a financial crisis. *"I had hardly any money in the bank because I never took what normally a 'positioned' CEO wage was."* She only wanted the money from the charity to be invested in the development of programs and workshops for the children and young people and to run the everyday affairs of the company. However, she has learned about resilience from her mother, her children gave her the strength to fight back so she managed to get her finances back on track through persistence.

Recommendations for Government and Young Indigenous Women Entrepreneurs

Fran thinks that the government provides a lot of money to large organizations but they do not provide the same support to small-scale entrepreneurs. *"As a company I didn't qualify, I had to get a Not-for-Profit status to apply for funding. In some circumstances your company had to have a threshold of a certain amount to even get them to look at me, I often didn't meet that threshold but I was still delivering workshops and trying to produce films. Small businesses struggle. I know of people that have actually left their much-loved businesses and close their doors due to a lack of support."*

Similarly, she believes that the government should provide support for young women entrepreneurs so that they can receive proper guidance and mentorship from Indigenous people who have great experiences to share. *"I think when people are starting out with their business they just need that Indigenous influence and support. There is a cultural understanding and cultural purpose that can give one more confidence to move forward and from action as we know 'from small things big things grow'.*

Conclusions

Fran Dobbie is a multi-talented and strong Aboriginal woman who has contributed immensely to the proud heritage of the Aboriginal community. Fran has played a positive role for her community in all her roles. She is truly inspirational and a role model for the young members of the community.

Education in the Aboriginal context goes back well before colonization, to what Bishop (2021) describes as a thriving education system that has always been "in place, from place." Further, Rigney (2015, as cited in Bishop, 2022) asserts, "curriculum didn't arrive on a boat, pedagogy didn't arrive on a boat, it was always here." However, education in contemporary Australia leads many children to fall behind due to systemic biases and disadvantages that remain inadequately addressed by government policy. The impact of this is severalfold, as not only are children, both Aboriginal and non-Aboriginal, deprived of culturally adept education, but they are left with the emotional impact of being coerced into compliance by a system that aims to indoctrinate and assimilate (Bishop, 2021).

As noted by O'Loughlin (2009), educators have the ability to provide "restorative therapeutic possibilities" for children and others. Fran's ability to utilise the power of storytelling, which dates back to the Dreamtime in Aboriginal history, allows her to educate and enrich her audience. As well as this, Fran's background in education and charity work gives her the necessary skills to be a powerful and effective communicator and educator through her current chosen medium of film. Fran's businesses are a means of supporting her community and giving a voice to our Indigenous sovereignty through art and education.

As O'Loughlin (2009) states, "*a teacher with a passion for myth, storytelling, drama, memory, and the Wisdom of Elders will draw these evocative knowledges.*" Fran Dobbie, as an Aboriginal woman, entrepreneur, mother, motivational speaker, producer, and writer harnesses the skills required from each role to successfully support her business and community.

References

Bishop, M. (2021). A rationale for the urgency of Indigenous education sovereignty: Enough's enough. *Australian Educational Researcher*, *48*(3), 419–432. https://doi.org/10.1007/s13384-020-00404-w

Bishop, M. (2022). Indigenous education sovereignty: Another way of 'doing' education. *Critical Studies in Education*, *63*(1), 131–146. https://doi.org/10.1080/17508487.2020.1848895

O'Loughlin, M. (2009). A Psychoanalytic exploration of collective trauma among indigenous Australians and a suggestion for intervention. *Australasian Psychiatry*, *17*(1_suppl), S33–S36. https://doi.org/10.1080/10398560902948746

12 Denni Francisco: Founder and Creative Director of Ngali

https://ngali.com.au/

Meena Chavan, Jane Menzies, and Leanne Holt

At Ngali, we take stunning First Nations' artwork beyond wall display and onto garments to walk the streets and show up in a myriad of places around the world. We strive to practice just-in-time manufacturing and offer an alternative to fast fashion. Using high-quality fabrics that last, means our pieces can be worn for the longest time, recycled and eventually up-cycled. Our collections are beyond trend and designed to move effortlessly through seasons and are styled for all occasions.

Denni Francisco and Ngali: A Journey of Culture, Creativity, and Community Impact

Ngali a multi award winning First Nations Fashion Brand.

Denni Francisco is the Founder and Creative Director of *Ngali*, an award-winning fashion label based in Melbourne, Victoria. As a proud Wiradjuri woman from New South Wales, Denni has made it her mission to use fashion as a platform to amplify Indigenous stories and culture. The ethos of Ngali—expressed through its tagline "together we create"—captures the spirit of collaboration with Indigenous Australian artists. Through these partnerships, Ngali translates Indigenous artworks into fashion garments that celebrate the richness of Aboriginal culture. Denni's achievements include winning the National Indigenous Fashion Design Award in 2021 and 2022, and she continues to pave the way for First Nations designers and artists to share their creativity with the world.

Denni established Ngali in September 2018, following a career in children's clothing as the former owner of Billiecart Clothing, and later in the corporate sector, running resilience training programs. Reflecting on her decision to launch Ngali, Denni shared, "It started because I missed the creative process and felt I could do more to support our First Nations communities. I missed getting out on country and connecting more with culture."

DOI: 10.4324/9781003386230-12

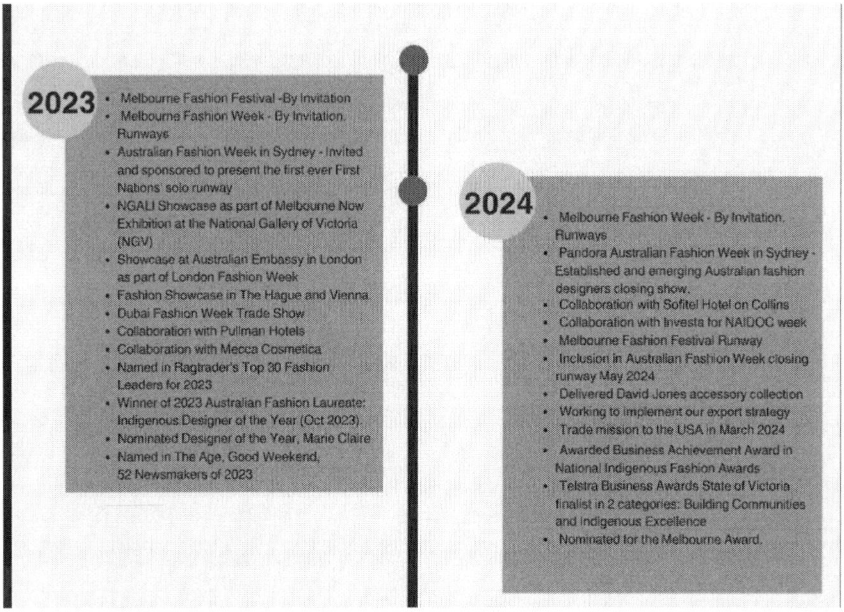

Figure 12.1 Ngali's 2023 and 2024 activities

"It's been an interesting ride, but it seems that our collections are well accepted," she continued. "It's providing a good opportunity to share culture and stories, and to celebrate who we are."

Denni views fashion not just as an industry but as a vehicle for conveying cultural narratives and identities. Her approach aligns with the work of Findlay and Card (2018), who argue that fashion acts as a symbolic medium, allowing wearers to embody and reproduce cultural stories through their everyday attire.

"I thought that the world didn't need another fashion brand unless it was meaningful," Denni explained. "For me, it was about how to use fashion as a platform to support First Nations artists and contribute to the education of our children in remote areas."

The name *Ngali*, meaning "we" or "us" in several Aboriginal languages, reflects the company's commitment to bringing Indigenous culture into the spotlight. Ngali garments, made with high-quality, sustainably sourced fabrics, symbolize the union between Country and people, honoring both the land and the individuals who inhabit it.

At its core, Ngali is dedicated to investing in Indigenous artists and contributing to Indigenous communities. This reinforces the argument that Indigenous businesses play a crucial role in supporting the well-being of their communities (Collins & Norman, 2018). Denni's sustainable business practices further reflect Indigenous cultural values, which regard the environment as sacred and invaluable (Chakraborty & Sadachar, 2023). Moreover, Denni's business functions as a site of social innovation, advancing these values through both its mission and its products (Findlay & Card, 2018).

Denni embraces the challenges of entrepreneurship, finding excitement in discovering new possibilities. "It's always challenging, but I enjoy the excitement of seeking out new possibilities and looking at what could be created that doesn't exist yet," she shared. "I love that part of entrepreneurship. I think it's a better way for me to contribute than just being employed at a company."

Her sense of fulfillment through the creative process aligns with research by Nikolaev and Wood (2020), who found a positive correlation between entrepreneurship and psychological well-being. Entrepreneurs in their study reported greater levels of self-acceptance, meaning, and fulfillment—demonstrating how engagement in business can enhance mental health and overall well-being.

Entrepreneurship offers flexibility, a quality Denni cherishes as a First Nations woman. "As a First Nations person, having freedom and not being confined is important," Denni reflected. "When you're out on country, there's this sense of freedom and guidance that comes from connection with our ancestors."

This sense of autonomy aligns with research by Magson et al. (2022), which suggests that autonomy in the workplace is closely linked to job satisfaction and work commitment, particularly for Indigenous people. Thus, the freedom afforded by entrepreneurship can enhance work satisfaction for First Nations business owners.

Denni's paternal grandmother played a pivotal role in her upbringing. "I was very close to her," she said. "The connection and stories that I have with culture come from her." Despite the challenges of running a business as a First Nations woman, Denni has not felt limited by her identity. However, she has faced challenges as a female entrepreneur, particularly with accessing funding. "When you think about the small percentages that support investment into female businesses, it is a barrier to accessing opportunities. I've certainly experienced that as a female rather than as a First Nations female right now," she explained.

Her experience echoes the findings of Strawser et al. (2021), who highlight that women, particularly Indigenous women, often face significant challenges in securing funding. These barriers to financial resources impede opportunities for women entrepreneurs and contribute to inequality in business ownership. Access to funding would not only mitigate these disparities but also stimulate the broader economy as women invest in their communities and develop financial literacy.

Denni's lighter skin tone means her Indigenous identity is not always immediately visible, and as a result, she does not face the same racial prejudices that some of her family members might. "I don't have the lived experience of being an obvious Indigenous Aboriginal person," she shared. "I don't push up against or feel the backlash of racial prejudice as much. My brothers probably got more than I did."

Despite these privileges, Denni acknowledges her responsibility to give back to her community. "I don't think I've been held back that way, and that's why I feel that I have a responsibility to do what I can to contribute to our community," she said.

Denni recognizes that First Nations entrepreneurs must often navigate business practices that do not align with their cultural values. "It's a struggle to try and fit into a US-centric way to do business," she explained. "Having to make a business plan, follow a template, and do things a certain way feels wrong. I just think, oh my gosh, I have it in my head in the same way, but putting all the boundaries and boxes around it feels like a very US-centric way of doing business. It doesn't feel right." For Denni, business is driven by intuition, feelings, and deep cultural connections, elements often overlooked in Western business practices.

This sentiment resonates with the work of Woods and Carroll (2022), who argue that Western business practices, with their focus on individualism and profit maximization, often disregard Indigenous knowledge systems and force Indigenous people to disconnect from their cultural ways of being. Denni, like many Indigenous entrepreneurs, believes that success is measured not by personal wealth but by the positive impact on her community. "What contribution am I making to our Indigenous artists and their communities?" she asks. "What contribution am I making to the royalties that get paid to artists or the education of kids?"

Denni's business, Ngali, embodies this relational approach to entrepreneurship, emphasizing community connections and contributions over individual gain. As a social enterprise, Ngali's *Buy 1, Give 1 Business for Good* initiative ensures that a portion of the profits from each garment sold supports young people in remote Indigenous communities to develop IT and literacy skills.

Denni's dream of expanding Ngali internationally is slowly becoming a reality. She has always envisioned taking Indigenous art off the walls of galleries and into the streets, using fashion as a platform to showcase First Nations' artworks globally. "We've been invited to participate in several runways during fashion weeks in places such as Milan in the last few years," she said. After winning the 2021 Fashion Design Award, Ngali was invited to present at Milan Fashion Week in 2022, a significant opportunity for international exposure.

Ngali's international presence continues to grow. In addition to its presence at Milan Fashion Week, the brand has showcased its collections at major Australian fashion events, including the Virgin Australia Melbourne Fashion Festival (VAMFF) in 2020 and Afterpay Australian Fashion Week (AAFW) in 2021.

Through these initiatives, Denni hopes to engage both Indigenous and non-Indigenous customers. For Indigenous customers, Ngali offers a chance to wear First Nations fashion with pride. For non-Indigenous customers, it serves as a gateway to learning about Indigenous culture. "For non-Indigenous customers, it's a soft entry to learn more about Indigenous culture. They may not have known much about the culture before, and this is a new way to explore, or they may already know, and it's an opportunity to support First Nations businesses," Denni explained.

Ngali's garments provide a means for people to connect with culture, supporting Findlay and Card's (2018) assertion that fashion is a medium through which individuals can express and engage with cultural identities.

Policy Implications

Denni's journey reinforces the importance of improving access to financial resources for women, particularly Indigenous women, to remove barriers to entrepreneurship (Strawser et al., 2021). Beyond the material benefits of starting a business, entrepreneurship can significantly enhance psychological well-being and work satisfaction, particularly when it offers the freedom to operate outside of traditional corporate structures (Magson et al., 2022; Nikolaev & Wood, 2020).

Indigenous knowledge systems and cultural practices must be valued and incorporated into entrepreneurial frameworks, policies, and programs. The imposition of Western business practices, which prioritize individualism and profit maximization, can alienate Indigenous entrepreneurs from their cultural ways of being and impede their success (Woods & Carroll, 2022). By recognizing and embracing Indigenous ways of doing business, policies can better support the flourishing of Indigenous entrepreneurship and its contributions to community well-being.

References

Chakraborty, S., & Sadachar, A. (2023). Can a connection with the Indigenous cultural values encourage sustainable apparel consumption? *Journal of Fashion Marketing and Management*, *27*(1), 80–99. https://doi.org/10.1108/JFMM-07-2021-0191

Collins, J., & Norman, H. (2018). Indigenous entrepreneurship and Indigenous employment in Australia. *Journal of Australian Political Economy*, *82*, 149–170. www.ppesydney.net/content/uploads/2020/05/Indigenous-entrepreneurship-and-indigenous-employment-in-Australia.pdf

Findlay, R., & Card, A. (2018). Introduction: Fashioning performance/performing dress. *About Performance*, *16*(1), 1–4.

Magson, R. G., Ryan, R. M., Dillon, A., Mooney, J., Blacklock, F., Yeung, A. S., Kadir, M. S., & Franklin, A. (2022). A cross-cultural investigation of basic psychological need satisfaction at work in an indigenous and non-indigenous Australian sample across occupation types. *Journal of Cross-Cultural Psychology*, *53*(2), 213–238. https://doi.org/10.1177/00220221211060441

Nikolaev, B., Boudreaux, C. J., & Wood, M. (2020). Entrepreneurship and subjective well-being: The mediating role of psychological functioning. *Entrepreneurship Theory and Practice*, *44*(3), 557–586. https://doi.org/10.1177/1042258719830314

Strawser, J. A., Hechavarría, D. M., & Passerini, K. (2021). Gender and entrepreneurship: Research frameworks, barriers and opportunities for women entrepreneurship worldwide. *Journal of Small Business Management*, *59*(sup1), S1–S15. https://doi.org/10.1080/00472778.2021.1965615

Woods, D., K., & Carroll, B. (2022). Decolonizing the business school: Reconstructing the entrepreneurship classroom through indigenizing pedagogy and learning. *Academy of Management Learning & Education*, *21*(1), 82–100. https://doi.org/10.5465/amle.2020.0366

13 Judith McDonald: A Journey of Determination, Advocacy and Entrepreneurship for Aboriginal Peoples

From Social Work to Social Impact Entrepreneur

www.watnandaconsulting.com.au/

Meena Chavan, Jane Menzies, and Leanne Holt

Watnanda was established with strong family values. These values include: treat everyone with respect and dignity, work hard, to value honesty, share knowledge, provide support and have gratitude. Watnanda is guided by our ancestors and Elders to ensure there is social justice and fairness for future Aboriginal and Torres Strait Islander generations to prosper and to be self-determining. Judy McDonald and Catherine Coysh are Gunditjmara women. Judy is currently based in the Southwest of Victoria, living on Gunditjmara Country, and Catherine is based in the Northeast of Victoria, living on Dhudhuroa Country. Judy began her small business as a sole trader in 2016, and then in 2019, Watnanda was reformed into a Company with Judy as the Managing Director and Catherine as the Corporate Director.

Watnanda works with service providers to deliver opportunities for social justice and fairness embedded in their day-to-day best practices and leadership. This can be achieved through

- having service providers with a safe level of cultural competency
- establishing and maintaining relationships
- provide a culturally safe environment
- working together in an equal partnership
- sharing information, providing choices, and allowing people to make informed decisions.

Watnanda offers social research, facilitation, and evaluation services to achieve the goals and outcomes that are required by all service providers under the Victorian Aboriginal Affairs Framework.

DOI: 10.4324/9781003386230-13

Social workers have long been the unsung heroes of society, advocating for the vulnerable, providing essential support services, and working tirelessly to address social inequities (Beresford, 2012).

However, the landscape of social services is evolving. Increasingly, social workers are harnessing their deep understanding of social issues to become social impact entrepreneurs, creating sustainable, scalable solutions that address the root causes of societal problems. This transformation not only broadens the scope of their impact but also brings innovative approaches to social change.

In an age where societal challenges are both abundant and complex, the role of the social worker has never been more critical. These dedicated professionals strive to improve the well-being of individuals and communities, tackling issues ranging from poverty to mental health.

However, as the landscape of social needs evolves, so too does the approach to addressing these challenges. Increasingly, social workers are transitioning into social impact entrepreneurs, blending their expertise in social issues with innovative business strategies to create sustainable and scalable solutions as in the case of our next Indigenous women entrepreneur – Judith McDonald.

As a social worker, she worked on the front lines of several societal issues. She worked in various settings, including schools, hospitals, non-profit organizations, and government agencies, addressing immediate needs and advocating for systemic change. Her training equipped her with a deep understanding of human behaviour, community dynamics, and social policies, which they use to support individuals and families in navigating life's challenges.

Judith McDonald is a proud Gunditjmara woman from the South-West of Victoria, currently living on Dhuduroa Country in North-East Victoria. Before starting her own business, Judy worked as a clinical social worker and in management within the health, justice, education, and community sectors. Throughout her career, she has passionately advocated for the self-determination and agency of rural and regional Aboriginal people; fighting for them to have a voice and for opportunities to achieve their goals.

In addition to her work at Watnanda Consulting, Judy currently serves on the Ovens Murray Aboriginal Governance Committee as Co-Chair, Victoria's Kinaway Chambers of Commerce Board, Albury Wodonga Health Ethics Committee, and the North-East Catchment Management Authority Board.

Judith possessed a unique set of skills that were directly transferable to social impact entrepreneurship. Her in-depth understanding of social issues, coupled with her experience in community engagement, made her well-equipped to identify needs and develop impactful solutions.

Her expertise and achievements within her industry have since been recognised through several awards. In 2015, she was inducted into the Victorian Aboriginal Honour Roll for her involvement in Aboriginal Affairs. In 2017, she was awarded an Honorary Doctorate of Letters from La Trobe University for her community work and contribution to research.

The traditional role of social workers involves direct service provision, case management, and advocacy. While these functions are indispensable, the increasing complexity of social problems requires solutions that go beyond immediate interventions. Enter the social impact entrepreneur.

A social impact entrepreneur is someone who creates and leads ventures that prioritize social good alongside financial sustainability. Unlike traditional entrepreneurs, whose primary focus is profit, social impact entrepreneurs aim to generate positive social change and address societal issues through innovative products, services, or processes (Fairlie & Fossen, 2020).

The transition from social worker to social impact entrepreneur involves leveraging a deep understanding of social issues to develop scalable and sustainable solutions. This shift requires a blend of empathy, business acumen, and a strategic mindset. Social impact entrepreneurs often employ business models that allow them to reinvest profits into their mission, ensuring long-term impact and growth and that is what we observed in the case of Judith.

Early Years

For Judy, starting her own business was a way to gain flexibility and autonomy over her career.

As she was finishing a twelve-month contract on Taskforce 1000 as the Senior Project Worker for the department of Health and Human Service in Ovens Murray and Goulburn areas– which looked at the systems and processes for Aboriginal kids in out-of-home care. Judy's role was to assist community organisations to work together, develop a strategy to implement that will improve the outcomes for Aboriginal children living in out of home care.

Judy's dad was living by himself and struggling. Judy built a granny flat at the back of her house for him to live in, but she wanted more time to take care of him during the day but still had to have an income. This is when starting up a business would resolve the matters that Judy was dealing with.

Previous literature identifies that entrepreneurship can often stem from necessity (Fairlie & Fossen, 2020) and having to deal with adverse and difficult situations (Menzies et al., 2024).

Judy thought about the types of work that had come across her desk over the years. "I thought, well, I could do that kind of work and look after my dad," she said. The flexibility of starting her own business meant that she could be with her dad during the day and do her work on the side."

"When I first went into business, I didn't have to spend much time advertising. I knew a lot of people in the northeast and my reputation was already built up," said Judy. "They knew that I was going into business, so I had lots of jobs lined up for me to do."

Success in social entrepreneurship often depends on a strong network of supporters, including mentors, investors, and collaborators. Social workers can leverage their existing professional networks and seek out new connections in the business and social innovation sectors.

"No one in my family had a business. Dad always worked on properties and mum took care of the house and our family. Mum was good at organising things and did a lot of volunteer work – fundraising. So, I've got some skills from mum and dad."

In terms of education, Judy dropped out of school after Form Three (year 9). "After I had my children, I went back to university as a mature age student and was the first one of my siblings to go to university, and the first one to start a business," she said. Judy currently holds a Bachelor of Social Work (undergraduate) and a Master of Social Work (postgraduate)– Research and an Honorary Doctorate for Letters from La Trobe University.

Starting Her Business

Social workers possess unique insights into the needs and gaps within their communities. Identifying a specific issue or population to focus on is the first step in creating a targeted and effective social venture.

Judy began her small business, Watnanda Consulting as a sole trader in 2017. Two years later, Watnanda incorporated to form the company, Watnanda Consulting Pty Ltd. Since then, she has held the position of Managing Director alongside her daughter, Catherine Coysh, Corporate Director. As a family business, Watnanda embodies strong family values through its leadership.

Across 11 different language groups on Gunditjmara Country, the word 'Watnanda' means 'together'. As one of the business' core principles, Watnanda symbolises the partnership between Judy's company and her clients to provide culturally responsive services. Watnanda specialises in social research, workshop facilitation and evaluation services to assist service providers to comply with their obligations under the Victorian Aboriginal Affairs Framework. This includes ensuring that service providers have safe levels of cultural competency and culturally safe environments. Further, Watnanda assists service providers to work alongside Indigenous communities in equal partnership by establishing and maintaining relationships. Lastly, Watnanda assists service providers to act with transparency and integrity by sharing information and allowing people to make informed decisions.

Watnanda's social research employs an Indigenous methodology framework to reflect Indigenous ways of knowing, being and doing. Guided by Black ethics and Social Work ethics, Watnanda's social research seeks to recognise and honour Indigenous world views and social norms. Privileging the voices of Aboriginal people and Aboriginal lands, the social research conducted by Watnanda places a strong emphasis on the underlying social, historical, and political contexts of Indigenous communities.

The consulting business also facilitates several workshops tailored to the specific needs of service providers. By undertaking a trauma-informed practice, the business facilitates truth-telling sessions that have been co-designed with its participants.

Challenges

Transitioning from social work to social impact entrepreneurship is not without its challenges. Social workers must often acquire new skills in business management, fundraising, and scaling operations. Additionally, they must navigate the tension between maintaining social missions and achieving financial sustainability. However, the potential for broader impact and systemic change provides a compelling incentive (Bornstein, 2007).

Funding is a critical component of any entrepreneurial venture. Social impact entrepreneurs can explore various funding sources, including grants, impact investments, crowdfunding, and social impact bonds but it is a challenge getting money.

Prevailing stereotypes and racist attitudes about Indigenous people have been a continual challenge for Judy. The stereotypes about Aboriginal people being lazy and drunk meant that Judy has always felt that she had to go above and beyond to prove that she was worthy.

"I can remember getting one contract and they never had never had an Aboriginal business before," said Judy. "They micromanaged me a lot." However, this was a great opportunity for her clients and for Judy as a business owner.

Through receiving mentorship and being guided through a framework of cultural practice principles, Judy has learned how to set boundaries and say no to things. She learnt how to say, "No, I don't think that fits with my values or principles," or "Yes, I would enjoy that, and it fits with my principles."

By unpacking and identifying her values and principles, Judy has been empowered to align her cultural identity with her work and values. Guided by her cultural values, Watnanda upholds values of respect and dignity, honesty, shared knowledge, hard work and support. Further, social justice and fairness for future Aboriginal and Torres Strait Islander generations are embedded into the company's values.

Success

Demonstrating the effectiveness of a social venture is crucial. Social impact entrepreneurs need to develop metrics and evaluation methods to measure their impact, ensuring transparency and accountability.

Having a strong reputation and respect within one's sector is how Judy measures success. "I was so excited when I got my first request, I was selected from around six other people or businesses." For her, being selected over six other candidates was proof that she was trusted and respected in her industry. "Being asked to be part of state-wide councils or state-wide advisory groups, that's another milestone in my business."

"The other milestone in my business was making over $75,000," said Judy. "It blew my mind that I could actually earn that amount of money."

On Entrepreneurship

For Judy, entrepreneurship isn't about making a profit and competing with other businesses. "What I think about entrepreneurs in Western terminology, it's foreign to me. I think it's about one of the principles – reciprocal," she said.

"If there's anything about competition, I'll run backwards. Business is about supporting one another to do able to do the work for our mob."

The transition from social worker to social impact entrepreneur required a shift in mindset from service provision to innovation and sustainability. Social workers may need to acquire new skills in business management, marketing, and finance. Additionally, balancing social missions with financial viability can be demanding.

However, the rewards are significant. Social impact entrepreneurs have the potential to create systemic change, addressing the root causes of social issues rather than merely treating symptoms. By scaling their solutions, they can reach a broader audience and achieve a greater impact than traditional social work methods alone.

Further Growth

As Judy comes to the end of her working life, her focus is shifting towards supporting growth and mentorship. "I think that I can share what I've learned with other people and share the knowledge and opportunities that I've had," she said.

"I'm putting opportunities up to the businesses that we've got around. We had some grant money that they could apply for, and I would talk them through applying for grants for their own businesses," said Judith. "Most of them are hustlers on the side. They're already employed but some of them have got this dream that they would like to start their own business."

Conclusions

The transition from social worker to social impact entrepreneur represents a powerful evolution in the quest to solve societal challenges. By combining the compassion and expertise of social work with the innovation and sustainability of entrepreneurship, these professionals are creating transformative change. As more social workers embrace this path, the potential for widespread social impact grows, heralding a future where business and social good are not only compatible but symbiotic.

Judith's story is one of resilience, empowerment, and leadership (Menzies et al., 2024).

Her work has not only advanced the interests of the Aboriginal community but has also set a benchmark for culturally responsive service provision. Through Watnanda Consulting, Judy has created a legacy that honours her heritage and paves the way for future generations. Her journey underscores the importance of cultural identity in professional endeavours and highlights the transformative power of entrepreneurship rooted in community values and principles. Judy's achievements serve as an inspiration, demonstrating that success is measured not just by financial gain but by the respect and trust one earns within their community and industry.

References

Beresford, P. (2012). What service users want from social workers. *Community Care*. Retrieved 30/03/2021 from www.communitycare.co.uk/2012/04/27/what-service-users-want-from-social-workers/

Bornstein, D. (2007). *How to Change the World: Social Entrepreneurs and the Power of New Ideas*. Oxford University Press.

Fairlie, R. W., & Fossen, F. M. (2020). Defining Opportunity versus Necessity Entrepreneurship: Two Components of Business Creation. In S. W. Polachek & K. Tatsiramos (Eds.), *Change at Home, in the Labor Market, and On the Job* (Vol. 48, pp. 253–289): Emerald Publishing Limited.

Menzies, J., Chavan, M., Jack, R., Scarparo, S., & Chirico, F. (2024). Australian indigenous female entrepreneurs: The role of adversity quotient. *Journal of Business Research, 175*, 114558. https://doi.org/10.1016/j.jbusres.2024.114558

14 Desert Gem: Vattessa Colbung's Resilient Path to Empowerment and Community Support

www.desertgem.com.au/

Meena Chavan, Jane Menzies, and Leanne Holt

Vattessa and her family are proud descendants of the Bibbulman nation belonging to Wagyl Kaip (the MINANG peoples of King George Sound) and Southwest Boojarah, located in Busselton.

Vattessa's connections to Goldfields are Wongatha nations through her (Tjalkatjarra people's) through Yilka Talintji in the Northern Goldfields 'her grandmother's country and (Tjerradjal peoples) Kakarra in the Central Eastern and Western, Goldfield's. She is the founder of *Desert Gem*, established in 2012. She is committed to challenging the status quo by empowering Indigenous Australians to realise their full potential and work toward a better future.

Both of Vattessa's parents were part of the "Stolen Generation." Her maternal grandparents were forcibly removed from their families, with her grandmother who was born at Erlistoun Station, where her mother Wadgeela (deceased), worked as a station hand. After working at Erlistoun Station, a Pastoral operated cattle station in Western Australia situated 72 kilometres to the north of Laverton. Her mother, Wadgeela (deceased), took her grandmother back to Cosmo Newberry, as her grandparents were the apical ancestors of that area. Our grandfather was removed from Karonie where his apical ancestors came from. The intergenerational trauma of these experiences profoundly impacted her upbringing, as it has for many Aboriginal people today. According to research, intergenerational trauma, stemming from settler-colonialism, continues to have lasting effects on the mental health and well-being of Aboriginal communities (Australian Institute of Health and Welfare, 2022; Menzies, 2019). Despite these challenges, Vattessa's family instilled a strong work ethic that ultimately opened doors for her in later life.

Her mother, Gwen Miller, an active member of the Aboriginal community, worked in the healthcare system for over thirty years to improve access to health services in Ceduna, South Australia. Vattessa admired her mother's community-oriented work and aspired to make a similar impact. "I had always helped out in the community, and I am very community-oriented," she

DOI: 10.4324/9781003386230-14

reflects. Vattessa also draws strength from her father's resilience, despite the difficult circumstances he faced also as a stolen generation father. Her step-father, Wayne Miller (deceased), too, played an influential role, working as the Chairperson of the Australian ATSIC Council of South Australia embodying the values of service and community engagement. Research highlights the positive influence that family role models can have on entrepreneurial success (Abbasianchavari & Moritz, 2021; Todd, 2012).

Education and Early Career

Vattessa in her younger years enjoyed school. Her education journey faced challenges. She dropped out of high school due to personal issues.

At sixteen, Vattessa entered the workforce, securing her first job at a Ceduna Bakery as a trainee where she managed daily operations while also being part of family responsibilities with the rest of her siblings. This early experience of balancing work and family life built a foundation for her resilience. She later pursued adult education programs, gaining certifications in hospitality, demonstrating her commitment to lifelong learning and professional growth.

While working in the hospitality industry, Vattessa drew on the values her grandmother taught her. She also worked as a receptionist and an Indigenous Support Officer in a local high school, where she mentored Aboriginal students, helping them stay engaged with their education. As she advanced in her career, Vattessa became more involved in initiatives focused on supporting Aboriginal communities, including working as a transport officer from 2006 to 2007 and later leading a smoke-free project across the Goldfields region within Western Australia. These experiences deepened her commitment to creating meaningful change within the Aboriginal community.

Entrepreneurship and Business

Vattessa founded *Desert Gem* in 2012, although she initially spent a few years laying the groundwork, building networks, and gaining insights into the challenges Aboriginal entrepreneurs face. During this time, she recognised a significant gap in support for released prisoners and began providing assistance to help them reintegrate into society. "A lot of things had changed from when they had gone into jail," she explains. "It was challenging working in these areas of supporting the men who wanted to return to jail because they couldn't handle society."

Juggling multiple roles as a business owner, community leader, and single mother presented significant challenges. The early years of running her online business, which sold contemporary Aboriginal artwork flip-flops (footwear), were especially tough. "Those years, it was very hard," she reflects. Finding a support network proved difficult, and Vattessa often had to rely on family for financial support. "You need that help, or you're literally doing it on your own," she says. Balancing business responsibilities with raising her children required perseverance and adaptability.

Despite these difficulties, Vattessa was determined to support other Indigenous entrepreneurs and provide financial assistance where she could. However, this effort also led to financial strain, resulting in a temporary closure of her business. Despite setbacks, Vattessa continued to offer guidance to emerging businesses in her community.

Challenges and Advocacy

Vattessa acknowledges the progress made for Aboriginal women in business today, yet challenges remain. "I don't think it is as hard today for Aboriginal women compared to when I started," she says, but adds that significant gaps still exist, particularly in wage equality. "Statistics show that Indigenous women are paid less than non-Indigenous women," she notes. She advocates for increased support from the Australian government to address these disparities and provide mentorship opportunities for Aboriginal women entrepreneurs.

One key area of focus is improving access to education, particularly for young Aboriginal girls who face barriers to completing school. "A lot of Aboriginal girls leave school early," she explains, emphasizing the need for programs that improve literacy and numeracy within Aboriginal communities. Vattessa stresses the importance of mentoring, support, and cultural awareness in overcoming these barriers.

Lessons Learned

Vattessa Colbung's journey offers invaluable lessons for aspiring entrepreneurs. First and foremost, her story highlights the power of resilience. Despite facing numerous challenges, including intergenerational trauma, Vattessa has used her experiences to fuel her drive for change. Her approach to business is rooted in service to the community, demonstrating that social enterprises can create positive societal impact alongside financial success.

Her story also emphasizes the importance of mentorship. Vattessa acknowledges the guidance she received from key figures in her life, particularly her mentors, Dawn Gilchrist and Dr. Charles Douglas, whose support was crucial in her career development. Research underscores the significance of mentorship and support networks for entrepreneurial success (Fredericks et al., 2021).

Vattessa's success also reflects the importance of cultural integrity in business. "Maintaining cultural integrity and using it as a foundation for business practices can lead to meaningful and sustainable entrepreneurship," she states. Her journey exemplifies the value of adapting to new roles, leveraging personal strengths, and fostering a growth mindset. As Vattessa's experiences demonstrate, entrepreneurs must be adaptable, innovative, and resilient in navigating the complexities of business.

Future Directions

Looking ahead, Vattessa envisions expanding *Desert Gem* with the support of partners like Many Rivers Microfinance, an organization committed to supporting Aboriginal communities. Their guidance in areas such as finance, marketing, and business coaching will help accelerate the growth of her business. Vattessa is also focused on starting small with creating employment opportunities for Indigenous Australians and contributing to environmental sustainability.

Her work continues to focus on empowering the next generation of Indigenous leaders and making lasting contributions to her community. Vattessa has since made many changes to her business from modelling program that empowered three Indigenous young females to prepare themselves for Kalgoorlie Fashion week 2017. Desert Gem is now a commercial supplier of the following:

- Biodegradable and Compostable Utensils.
- Premium Yarn & Bush coffee bean blends.
- Automated electronic coffee machine rental hire or buy.
- Solar Powered Lighting Tower rental hire.

Conclusion

Vattessa Colbung's journey is a powerful testament to the resilience, strength, and transformative potential of Indigenous entrepreneurs. Through her business, *Desert Gem*, and her extensive past work in community service, Vattessa has proven that adversity can be transformed into a catalyst for positive change. Her ongoing commitment to empowering Aboriginal communities, particularly women and youth, provides a valuable model for social entrepreneurship. Vattessa's story not only inspires others to persevere in the face of challenges but also offers a blueprint for creating businesses that serve both social and economic needs. Her legacy is one of empowerment, healing, and hope for future generations.

References

Abbasianchavari, A., & Moritz, A. (2021). The impact of role models on entrepreneurial intentions and behavior: A review of the literature. *Management Review Quarterly, 71*(1), 1–40. doi:10.1007/s11301-019-00179-0

Australian Institute of Health and Welfare. (2022). Indigenous health and wellbeing. Accesed on 02/06/2023, Retrieved from www.aihw.gov.au/reports/australias-health/indigenous-health-and-wellbeing

Fredericks, B., Daniels, C., Kinnear, S., & Mikecz, M. (2021). The mentor experience: Mentoring for Indigenous Australian school to university success. *Journal of Australian Indigenous Issues, 24,* 3–21. https://search.informit.org/doi/pdf/10.3316/informit.046651292466851?download=true

Menzies, K. (2019). Understanding the Australian Aboriginal experience of collective, historical and intergenerational trauma. *International Social Work, 62*(6), 1522–1534. doi:10.1177/0020872819870585

Todd, R. (2012). Young urban Aboriginal women entrepreneurs: Social capital, complex transitions and community support. *British Journal of Canadian Studies, 25*(1), 1–19,149.

15 Janine McDonald: Empowering Aboriginal Employment at All Aspects Recruitment and HR Services

www.aarecruit.com.au/

Meena Chavan, Jane Menzies, and Leanne Holt

All Aspects is an Aboriginal owned and operated business based in Darwin, in the Northern Territory and Queensland.

Janine McDonald is the Director of *All Aspects Recruitment and HR Services*, a company dedicated to improving employment outcomes for Aboriginal Australians and breaking the links from welfare dependency. With over two decades of experience in recruitment, Janine has been a tireless advocate for Aboriginal employment and has served as a role model in the private sector and government settings. Her company's mission is "people first every time", reflecting her commitment to creating meaningful and sustainable employment opportunities for Aboriginal Australians. This aligns with broader research that highlights the social impact of Aboriginal businesses in Australia, particularly those focused on benefiting their communities (Morley, 2014).

Early Life and Personal Background

Janine was born in South Australia where neither of her parents had received a higher level of education. As she reflects, "My father had approximately four years of schooling, and my mother attended public high school." Her parents worked in the public sector before venturing into their own business. Growing up, Janine and her sister were heavily involved in their parents' service station where their parents worked tirelessly. From a very young age, Janine and her sister supported their parent's businesses before and after school and weekends, which instilled in them a strong understanding of good commercial practices.

While she initially had no intention of entering the business world herself, the experience taught her valuable lessons about hard work and business leadership. "I thought it was just the environment I grew up in, working seven days a week for 15 hours a day. It was a lot of work," Janine reflects. However, over time she recognized the positive influence her parents had on her, shaping her understanding of resilience and business leadership. Research suggests that

DOI: 10.4324/9781003386230-15

role models, like her parents, play a crucial role in shaping the aspirations and entrepreneurial journeys of young people (Abbasianchavari & Moritz, 2021).

Professional Career in Government

After completing high school, Janine began working in the Commonwealth of Australia Government and focusing on Indigenous Affairs. Commencing in the Pitjantjatjara region, she transferred to Western Australia which then involved extensive travel and significant responsibilities, working closely with the Elected Councils. "It was crazy—we travelled extensively in the Western Desert/Wongatha Regions, and I thought I'd achieved a good life balance."

After relocating to the Northern Territory, Janine's mentor left, which changed everything for her. This shift gave Janine the opportunity to stand up and take a lead role to drive Aboriginal careers from within the public sector, a chance she embraced passionately. "I was shocked to see a lot of our mob; Aboriginal people all stuck in APS Level 1 and 2 positions, and I thought, why aren't we doing more to helping people to progress and grow particularly in Aboriginal affairs?" This sense of purpose became a driving force for Janine, and she worked tirelessly to support her colleagues and facilitate career growth among Aboriginal Australians.

Following the closure of Aboriginal & Torres Strait Islander Commission (ATSIC), Janine moved to a similar role in another department, continuing to champion Aboriginal career development. "I supported everyone as much as I could, and I worked hard to move Aboriginal people upwards and this was achieved by supporting their journey through training and mentoring. To me, placing Aboriginal individuals in high-profile roles was a strategic and valuable endeavour as it was a need and gap to ensure their voices were being heard at the table. Allowing them to contribute from their own experiences and perspectives."

Founding All Aspects Recruitment and HR Services

While working in the public sector, Janine began to notice certain limitations that hindered progress in Aboriginal employment. She recognized that there was untapped potential within the Aboriginal community and that gaps in support systems were impeding greater achievements. "We weren't progressing with Aboriginal empowerment or employment as much as we could have. There were a lot of gaps still," she reflects.

This realization, paired with her desire to have a more direct impact, led Janine to consider launching her own recruitment agency. She was introduced to a General Manager through a mutual friend of an international recruitment agency who had over 30 years of experience in Australia's industrial relations and financial sector. The two quickly recognized their complementary skills and commenced their journey to start *All Aspects Recruitment and HR Services.*

The company's mission is clear: to place more Aboriginal people into meaningful employment by matching their skill sets to available opportunities. "We ensure that all candidates have met the required checks before placements". If we're placing someone in a remote community, cultural competence is essential," says Janine.

Her dedication to the business is fuelled by a deep passion for creating lasting change. "It takes a lot of guts and commitment," she notes. "My reputation is everything. It takes a lifetime to build, and only a second to crumble." So we know it is up to us to ensure we are accountable to legislations and obligations.

Janine's family has been integral to the business's success. Her oldest daughter, Danielle, worked alongside her for nine months, and her other daughter Casey, contributed on a part-time arrangement that assisted us establish our company. A very supporting partner that continually encouraged and took on all the other responsibilities to allow Janine to concentrate on achieving outcomes "Having a family that believes in your dreams is incredible," Janine says. "Their support was the key motivator for me."

Overcoming Challenges

Transitioning from a government role to running a private business posed a significant change. Janine jokes about her shift from a "precious princess" to becoming all the gaps in your own business like the cleaner, the marketing manager, and or the office manager, besides being a Director. However, she acknowledges the importance of collaboration with her business partner Annette, who had high-level strengths across industrial relations and financial management. "It's a partnership, a friendship and a sister-hood, and it takes work within to maintain the relationship from both sides to earn and retain that respect and honesty."

Financial constraints also present ongoing challenges. In particular, the annual costs of renewing memberships across multiple states and dealing with legal and regulatory requirements have created financial strain. "To get legal advice for a $20,000 contract could cost a business $5,000" she notes, underscoring the business's vulnerability to legal and financial pressures. Economic volatility, particularly during the periods of financial downturn, further exacerbated these challenges. Despite this, Janine and Annette have resisted downsizing, preferring to maintain their staff and treat them like family.

Another obstacle Janine faces is what she calls "black cladding," a practice where non-Aboriginal businesses (or white businesses) partner with Aboriginal individuals solely to access government grants and contracts. "It's unethical and misuses public funding that should benefit Aboriginal businesses," she asserts.

Additionally, managing IT infrastructure and dealing with frequent scams and viruses are ongoing operational concerns. "We have to be vigilant and back up our systems constantly," and put other complimentary strategies in place she explains.

Growth and Expansion

Janine has considered expanding the business, but she remains cautious due to the risk management involved and takes into consideration every scenario that needs to be covered. Janine states – "you can't chase or take on everything but more so concentrate on your core skills and keep on track with your business direction." Reflecting back on the journey so far, Janine talks about the economic downturn around the world, the closure of major projects, the Covid-19 period and how the Directors strategically positioned themselves to ensure they maintained a good operating business financially.

Taking on the leadership of recruitment strategies across multiple communities, non-for-profit organisations, government placements and the private sector has demonstrated the growth, strength and delivery of our services. This displays our capabilities and reputation follow. The most important thing for me in this business is getting people into jobs, and supporting our clients and assisting them during periods of staffing shortages, new projects and restructures," she says. The company's focus remains on creating positive social impact – job outcomes and assisting individuals in securing employment that benefits not just them, but their families, friends and communities.

As a business owner you need to have an established network, be aware of upcoming projects, funding and programme delivery. As a small business you are that person that has to research, analyse, respond to establish yourself on those platforms.

"We sometimes spend days at forums and meetings with no revenue coming in," Janine points out. "So you have to weigh up what is the advantage of attending these events versus the loss of productivity whilst you are away."

Recommendations for the Next Generation

Janine believes that young people today have the tools and resources to become successful entrepreneurs, but they need the right support and guidance. "Starting a business is overwhelming. You can lie awake at night worrying about unpaid bills or whether you'll be able to keep your staff. It's important to ask questions and seek clarity," she advises.

She also encourages young people to develop a lifelong quest for knowledge. "To maintain a business, you need to stay informed about technology, marketing, legal obligations, the market and know finance/cash flows. Continual educating yourself is "the key to success."

Policy Recommendations

With her extensive experience working with government agencies, Janine believes that while policies like the Indigenous Procurement Policy (IPP) have made strides, there is still much work to be done. "The policy exists, but many government people in the remote regions have never heard of it," even though it was released in 2015, she says. She advocates for more effective dissemination of information to ensure the policy reaches the grassroots level. Additionally, Janine calls for better awareness and education on the national directory like *Supply Nation* with a vision of a prosperous, vibrant and sustainable Indigenous business sector, ensuring that the system operates with integrity and not to lose sight of what it is about.

Conclusion

Looking ahead, Janine hopes to retire as they had reached their 15-year anniversary. Her goal is to ensure that *All Aspects Recruitment and HR Services* continues to thrive even after her departure. "I'd love to see another Indigenous business take over," she says and takes it to another level again.

For Janine, the true reward of her work is not financial success, but the positive impact on individuals and communities.

"We never wanted to be the biggest recruitment company. We wanted to make a difference" — **and we have**," she concludes.

References

Abbasianchavari, A., & Moritz, A. (2021). The impact of role models on entrepreneurial intentions and behavior: A review of the literature. *Management Review Quarterly*, *71*(1), 1–40. https://doi.org/10.1007/s11301-019-00179-0

Morley, S. (2014). *Success Factors for Indigenous Entrepreneurs and Community-Based Enterprises*. Closing the Gap Clearinghouse. Retrieved 1/01/ 2024 from https://apo.org.au/sites/default/files/resource-files/2014-04/apo-nid39458.pdf

16 Lessons Learned, Policy Implications and Conclusions

Meena Chavan, Jane Menzies, and Leanne Holt

This final chapter synthesizes the key insights and lessons from the book, while also exploring the policy recommendations offered by Indigenous Women Entrepreneurs to stakeholders who can support and foster their entrepreneurial endeavours. These stakeholders include governments, organizations, and communities. Additionally, we examine the potential role of business associations and support networks in facilitating Indigenous Women's entrepreneurship.

Overall Findings

To summarize the core insights from this book, we present a word cloud that highlights the central themes prevalent throughout the participants' stories (Figure 16.1).

As the word cloud indicates, *community* was a prominent theme mentioned by many participants. For many of these women, serving their Indigenous community was at the heart of their business ventures. Many were deeply involved in promoting Indigenous rights within their communities. One participant, whose father was an Aboriginal activist in Redfern, NSW, grew up influenced by his advocacy for Aboriginal rights which was passed down to her. Through her business, she was able to offer cultural training to large corporations in Australia, helping them build cultural understanding of Indigenous peoples, which further helped in advocating for Indigenous rights in Australia, and providing a more inclusive environment within Australian organisations. This demonstrates the collective and individual agency that Indigenous peoples engage in to improve their situation, have a voice and advance the rights of their communities (Bandura, 2018). It underscores the agentic and advocate roles that many Indigenous women entrepreneurs assume.

Most participants in this study operated businesses that reflected their Aboriginal culture, emphasizing their desire to support their communities or align with their cultural values. These businesses encompassed a range of products and services, including Indigenous fashion, art, education, recruitment, entrepreneurship, gifts, films, music, and food. This diversity reflects how Indigenous women entrepreneurs value their cultural and spiritual

DOI: 10.4324/9781003386230-16

Figure 16.1 Word Cloud of Key Terms and Themes

connections to the land, which contributes positively to their overall well-being (AIHW, 2022). Many also aimed to facilitate organizations and individuals in working effectively with the Aboriginal community. The findings demonstrate the importance of cultural embeddedness for Indigenous peoples, highlighting that entrepreneurship is deeply influenced by cultural contexts, values, and norms (Ojong et al., 2021).

Several participants had experienced the trauma of the Stolen Generations or came from families affected by forced removals, which led to significant intergenerational trauma. Some participants were unaware of their Indigenous heritage, having grown up in white families, only to later discover their Aboriginal roots. For some individuals, such as Nicole Monks, artistic endeavours through her business allowed them to reconnect with her cultural heritage and family background.

The Indigenous women entrepreneurs in this study faced the dual challenges of being Indigenous and female in a society that often marginalized them. Many overcame personal struggles, including domestic violence, substance abuse, divorce, and depression. Some faced lateral violence (Australian Human Rights Commission, 2011) in their own Indigenous communities, with others often being jealous of their success, direct violence, ridicule and abuse to them. Some had established businesses not only to provide for their families but also because the corporate world often failed to accommodate their needs. These women also grappled with the stigma of being

"Aboriginal women in Australia," which eroded their self-esteem. Despite these challenges, they remained resilient, using their businesses as a source of strength and healing. As one participant shared, her business helped her cope with depression.

Participants also spoke of enduring prejudice and discrimination, both in society and within the justice system, which compounded the trauma they experienced. One participant recounted the difficulty of working in corporate Australia, where her Aboriginal heritage was met with skepticism and criticism. This persistent racism motivated some Indigenous women to leave corporate environments and, out of necessity, pursue entrepreneurship (Fairlie & Fossen, 2020).

Despite these challenges, participants reported receiving significant support from their communities and families. For example, Mundanara Bayles' family and their background in advocating for Indigenous people's rights was instrumental in fostering a supportive and thriving community, which allowed her to easily connect with other Indigenous peoples, and develop a very successful cultural training business. Her family, and her background also placed immense pressure on her to live up to expectations.

Many of the businesses explored in this study had found success, often due to the participants' prior professional experiences in the corporate or government sectors. This background enabled them to transfer valuable skills, business acumen, and corporate networks to their entrepreneurial ventures. It became evident that many of these women had experienced hardships during their formative years, which fuelled their determination. As a result, they developed a strong ability to cope with adversity—an important trait that contributed to their entrepreneurial success (Stoltz, 1997; Stoltz, 2004). This resilience, drive, and endurance were crucial factors in their ability to overcome business setbacks (Menzies et al., 2024).

Despite the obstacles they faced, the participants offered a range of practical and policy suggestions to better support Indigenous female entrepreneurs.

Practical and Policy Implications

1. Support in the First Six Months of Business

Several participants highlighted the challenges faced during the early stages of business, particularly in the first six months to two years, when doubts about the viability of their ventures often arose. To address this, government organisations such as Indigenous Business Australia (IBA) or Indigenous business associations, such as Kinaway in Victoria, could develop programs that provide mentorship and support to newly established businesses. This could include monthly one-on-one meetings with successful mentors to help build resilience, identify roadblocks, and provide guidance. Additionally, providing adversity training would help these entrepreneurs strengthen their ability to cope with setbacks (Menzies et al., 2024; Stoltz, 1997; Stoltz, 2004).

2. Strengths-Based and Culturally Safe Training
Despite progress, many Indigenous women still face racism. For example, some participants experienced comments such as "you're too white and pretty to be Indigenous" or faced teasing during childhood for their darker skin. Such experiences emphasize the need for culturally safe, strengths-based training that empowers women to address racism and discrimination effectively (Bryant et al., 2021). This training should focus on building resilience and increasing participants' agency in confronting negative remarks. Additionally, adversity quotient (AQ) training could help Indigenous women entrepreneurs navigate the challenges posed by their personal experiences with racism, sexism, and trauma (Stoltz, 1997; Stoltz, 2004). Strengths-based training empowers individuals by focusing on their positive attributes, skills, and potential, fostering confidence and motivation (Kennedy et al., 2022).

Culturally safe training, which respects and values Indigenous knowledge and practices, is crucial for Indigenous women entrepreneurs. Such programs help them pursue their economic goals and contribute to their communities while honouring their cultural identity (Kennedy et al., 2022). Moreover, government initiatives should continue to increase the representation of Indigenous professionals across various industries while fostering cultural sensitivity within institutions to enhance trust.

3. Integrating Entrepreneurship Education into Primary and Secondary Schools
A common recommendation from participants was to incorporate entrepreneurship education into primary and secondary school curricula across Australia, especically in locations where there is a greater density of Indigenous students. This would equip children with essential skills such as creativity, problem-solving, financial literacy, and critical thinking, which can foster an entrepreneurial mindset (Maritz & Foley, 2018). For example, Carol Vale shared a story about her grandchildren engaging in entrepreneurship through a business initiative, highlighting the importance of instilling entrepreneurial thinking at a young age.

This approach not only prepares children for future business endeavours but also encourages them to pursue their passions and contribute positively to society, thus breaking cycles of poverty and creating new economic opportunities.

4. Addressing Education to Enhance Indigenous Workforce Participation
A key recommendation from participants highlighted the need for improved educational opportunities to address the shortage of trained Aboriginal individuals in organizations, which negatively impacts the productivity of Indigenous businesses. One participant noted that access to education remains a significant barrier for Indigenous Australians pursuing entrepreneurial ventures, with a need for tailored education at different stages of life. She emphasized, "As much as I love the idea of tertiary education, what you need when you're older can be quite different from what's required when you're younger." She mentioned a valuable course she completed at Curtin University called 'Growth,' a 12-month program that only required one day of attendance each

month, offering essential support for her business alongside her studies. The recommendation is clear: there is a need to explore educational models that empower Indigenous women to upskill and enhance their entrepreneurial capabilities.

5. Building Networks, Role Models, and Mentorship Opportunities
Participants also underscored the importance of government support and confidence-building training for First Nations women, who often face self-doubt due to stereotypes and a lack of opportunities. One participant shared, "We tend to undersell ourselves, so I think the government needs to be more proactive in encouraging Indigenous women into these roles because, most of the time, we don't put ourselves forward."

Further, there is a call for targeted coaching programs that assess individual skill gaps, with Rachelle Towart highlighting the importance of identifying these gaps early. "Young people starting a business need to understand what skills they lack to reach their goals," she said.

As demand grows for Indigenous-owned businesses, the government should foster Indigenous-specific business education programs that are culturally sensitive and incorporate Indigenous knowledge systems.

Jenifer Daar believes that the community would benefit from more Indigenous entrepreneurial role models. "We need more Indigenous entrepreneurs to show the way," she said. Similarly, Kaylene emphasized the need for not only funding but also a robust support network to help sustain businesses. "If a business isn't sustainable, it won't survive to produce role models," she observed. Fran Dobbie added that government support for young female entrepreneurs, coupled with mentorship from experienced Indigenous individuals, is crucial. "Young entrepreneurs need that Indigenous influence to build confidence before they can expand into other arenas," she said.

The creation of Indigenous Women Entrepreneurship Networks was also discussed, with Jenifer Daar noting that, while her own network grew organically through years in the healthcare industry, formal networks are essential for emerging entrepreneurs. "National-level support might be invaluable for future entrepreneurs," she reflected.

Sharon shared her experience of creating a supportive online community where people could connect and share resources. "By offering a space for people to help each other, it becomes easier to navigate the entrepreneurial journey," she explained.

This emphasis on social networks and cultural connections aligns with research suggesting that such engagement enhances entrepreneurs' well-being and fosters better mental health outcomes (Murrup-Stewart et al., 2021).

Several Indigenous Women's Networks are already in existence, such as:

- **The National Aboriginal and Torres Strait Islander Women's Alliance (NATSIWA)**: Empowering Aboriginal and Torres Strait Islander women since 2009.

- **Wiyi Yani U Thangani (Women's Voices)**: A project launched in 2017 to engage with Indigenous women and girls and capture their stories and aspirations (Gubana & Wellauer, 2020).
- **Indigenous Business Australia's "Strong Women, Strong Business" network**, which provides mentorship and business knowledge-sharing opportunities (Indigenous Business Australia, 2024).

6. Creating Dedicated Spaces for Indigenous People

Nicole Monks proposed that cities and councils should create designated spaces for Indigenous communities to express their culture and share their stories, similar to the way many cities have 'Chinatowns.' This would provide a platform for the Indigenous population to practice and celebrate their culture in urban spaces.

7. Reforming the Indigenous Procurement Policy

A common sentiment among participants was the need to address the shortcomings of the Indigenous Procurement Policy (IPP) (Australian Government, 2024). While the policy mandates that Indigenous businesses tender for government contracts, many have found these processes frustratingly ineffective. One participant remarked, "The government needs to move beyond tick-box exercises in policies like the IPP."

Moreover, some participants felt that the IPP should offer more than entry-level opportunities. "We need to ensure that Indigenous people can access higher-level roles, not just entry-level positions," stated another participant. This view stresses the need for a more inclusive and accessible procurement policy for all Indigenous individuals across different career stages.

8. Encouraging Indigenous Women in Leadership Roles

There were strong calls for the government to focus on the development of leadership capabilities among Indigenous women. Despite the presence of some Indigenous women in lower-level roles, there remains significant room for growth at higher levels of leadership. Participants highlighted the need for increased representation of Indigenous women on boards and in senior management positions. One participant emphasized, "We need more Indigenous women at the board level and in senior management positions. There is little representation of First Nations women in these areas, and we must advocate for their inclusion."

9. Addressing Racism and Changing Public Perceptions

Racism remains a significant barrier to success for Indigenous businesswomen, with some participants noting that identifying as an Indigenous business can hinder access to contracts. "Some businesses have distanced themselves from their Aboriginal identity because it negatively impacts their chances of winning tenders," one participant shared.

Amanda Healy recounted a 30% decline in her business once she registered with Supply Nation (2024), pointing to the racial biases that persist in Australian society. These biases can affect business opportunities for

Indigenous entrepreneurs, underscoring the need for top-down reform to shift public attitudes and improve trust in Aboriginal businesses.

10. Improving Access to Funding and Loans for Indigenous Entrepreneurs
There was widespread consensus on the need to improve financial support for Indigenous women entrepreneurs, particularly through grants or loans that require less collateral. Many Indigenous women, especially older entrepreneurs who may have experienced personal hardship, face challenges in accessing traditional funding. One participant observed, "Indigenous entrepreneurs need access to funding that doesn't place unreasonable risk on the individual."

Participants also critiqued the lack of support for small-scale businesses, with one pointing out, "Large organizations receive substantial government funding, but small businesses often miss out due to high qualification criteria."

11. Enhancing Financial Literacy for Indigenous Women
Building financial literacy was identified as a crucial element in supporting Indigenous women entrepreneurs. Financial illiteracy, often passed down through generations, can deter women from pursuing business opportunities. To address this, participants recommended implementing financial literacy education programs from an early age, as well as providing ongoing support for women as they navigate their entrepreneurial journey.

12. Valuing Indigenous Knowledge in Business Practices
Finally, the integration of Indigenous knowledge systems into entrepreneurial practices was highlighted as essential for success. One participant remarked that Indigenous people have a long history of business and trade practices that should be acknowledged in entrepreneurship education. "We've been traders for thousands of years; our system of governance is embedded in our culture," she said. This knowledge should be incorporated into business curricula, both for Indigenous students and for all Australians.

In conclusion, the recommendations provided by Indigenous women entrepreneurs emphasize the need for greater support in the early stages of business, culturally safe training programs, and the incorporation of entrepreneurship education into schools. These steps are crucial in fostering a more inclusive and empowering entrepreneurial environment for Indigenous women.

Conclusions

This book celebrates the resilience and entrepreneurial spirit of Indigenous women entrepreneurs in Australia. Their stories of success, despite the challenges they face, serve as an inspiration to the broader Indigenous business community. By acknowledging their struggles and advocating for the systemic changes outlined in these recommendations, we can empower future generations of Indigenous women to succeed as entrepreneurs. Their contributions to both the cultural preservation and economic empowerment of Indigenous communities are invaluable. As we look to the future, it is essential that we continue to create pathways for these women to thrive, ensuring that their legacy will inspire many more to come.

References

AIHW. (2022). Profile of Indigenous Australians. Accesed on 05/05/22, Retrieved from www.aihw.gov.au/reports/australias-welfare/profile-of-indigenous-australians

Australian Government. (2024. Indigenous Procurement Policy. Accesed on Retrieved from www.niaa.gov.au/indigenous-affairs/economic-development/indigenous-procurement-policy-ipp

Australian Human Rights Commission. (2011). Chapter 2: Lateral violence in Aboriginal and Torres Strait Islander communities – Social Justice Report 2011. Accesed on 31/01/2025, Retrieved from https://humanrights.gov.au/our-work/publications/chapter-2-lateral-violence-aboriginal-and-torres-strait-islander-communities#:~:text=Lateral%20violence%2C%20also%20known%20as,shaming

Bandura, A. (2018). Toward a Psychology of Human Agency: Pathways and reflections. *Perspectives on Psychological Science, 13*(2), 130–136. doi:10.1177/1745691617699280

Bryant, J., Bolt, R., Botfield, J. R., Martin, K., Doyle, M., Murphy, D., ...Aggleton, P. (2021). Beyond deficit: 'Strengths-based approaches' in Indigenous health research. *Sociology of Health & Illness, 43*(6), 1405–1421.
https://doi.org/10.1111/1467-9566.13311

Fairlie, R. W., & Fossen, F. M. (2020). Defining Opportunity versus Necessity Entrepreneurship: Two Components of Business Creation. In S. W. Polachek & K. Tatsiramos (Eds.), *Change at Home, in the Labor Market, and On the Job* (Vol. 48, pp. 253–289). Emerald Publishing Limited.

Gubana, B., & Wellauer, K. (2020). Aboriginal women Landmark report 'Wiyi Yani U Thangani' released into challenges and goals of First Nations women and girls. Accesed on Retrieved from www.abc.net.au/news/2020-12-10/june-oscar-wiyi-yani-u-thangani-womens-voices-report-launched/12967564

Indigenous Business Australia. (2024). Strong Women Strong Business. Retrieved 26/02/2024 from https://iba.gov.au/business/strong-women-strong-business/

Kennedy, A., Sehgal, A., Szabo, J., McGowan, K., Lindstrom, G., Roach, P., ... Barnabe, C. (2022). Indigenous strengths-based approaches to healthcare and health professions education – Recognising the value of Elders' teachings. *Health Education Journal, 81*(4), 423–438. doi:10.1177/00178969221088921

Maritz, A., & Foley, D. (2018). Expanding Australian Indigenous Entrepreneurship Education Ecosystems. *Administrative Sciences, 8*(2). doi:10.3390/admsci8020020

Menzies, J., Chavan, M., Jack, R., Scarparo, S., & Chirico, F. (2024). Australian indigenous female entrepreneurs: The role of adversity quotient. *Journal of Business Research, 175*, 114558. doi:https://doi.org/10.1016/j.jbusres.2024.114558

Murrup-Stewart, C., Whyman, T., Jobson, L., & Adams, K. (2021). "Connection to culture is like a massive lifeline": Yarning with aboriginal young people about culture and social and emotional wellbeing. *Quality Health Research, 31*(10), 1833–1846. doi:10.1177/10497323211009475

Ojong, N., Simba, A., & Dana, L.-P. (2021). Female entrepreneurship in Africa: A review, trends, and future research directions. *Journal of Business Research, 132*, 233–248. doi:10.1016/j.jbusres.2021.04.032

Stoltz, P. G. (1997). *Adversity Quotient: Turning Obstacles into Opportunities.* Wiley.

Stoltz, P. G. (2004). Building resilience for uncertain times. *Leader to Leader, 2004*(31), 16–20. doi:https://doi.org/10.1002/ltl.58

Supply Nation. (2024). About Us. Retrieved 26/02/2024 from https://supplynation.org.au/about-us/our-mission/

Index

Printed in the United States
by Baker & Taylor Publisher Services